WRITERS AND THEIR WORK

ISOBEL ARMSTRONG
General Editor

JOHN FOWLES

D1135949

JOHN FOWLES

WW

JOHN FOWLES

William Stephenson

Northcote House
in association with the
British Council

To Sarah

'because of that fused rare power
that was her essence'

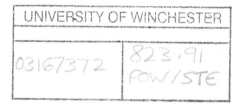

© Copyright 2003 by William Stephenson

First published in 2003 by Northcote House Publishers Ltd, Horndon, Tavistock, Devon, PL19 9NQ, United Kingdom.
Tel: +44 (01822) 810066. Fax: +44 (01822) 810034.

British Library Cataloguing-in-Publication Data
A catalogue record for this book is available from the British Library

ISBN 0-7463-1019-6 hardback
ISBN 0-7463-0987-2 paperback

Typeset by TW Typesetting, Plymouth, Devon
Printed and bound in the United Kingdom by
Athenaeum Press Ltd., Gateshead, Tyne & Wear

Contents

Acknowledgements

I would like to thank John Fowles for giving permission to quote from his work. I am also indebted to Sarah Fowles for her help, and to John Fowles's agent, Katie McKay of Gillon Aitken Associates, London. I am grateful to Aurum Press, Ltd, London, for permission to quote from *The Tree*, in particular to Piers Burnett for his help. Catherine Trippett of The Random House Archive and Library, Rushden, Northants., also gave invaluable assistance. Bruce Woodcock and Alistair Stead kindly agreed to read the manuscript at an early stage, and suggested many improvements; any remaining errors are, of course, mine. I am grateful to Ian Mortimer, Madeleine Midgley, and the staff of Exeter University Library, Special Collections, for their help with the unpublished manuscripts of John Fowles. My colleagues at Chester College of Higher Education (and previously at the Universities of Leeds, Hull, and Central Lancashire) have given me many useful insights for the book, as have my students. Finally, I am grateful to Brian Hulme at Northcote House for his help as editor, and to Isobel Armstrong for commissioning this study.

Biographical Outline

1926	John Robert Fowles born at Leigh-on-Sea, Essex, 31 March. Son of Robert, a tobacco importer, and Gladys (formerly Richards).
1939	Attends Bedford School. Autumn 1941, has nervous breakdown and returns home. Recovers completely. 1943, appointed head boy. Leaves 1944.
1940	Fowles family evacuated to Ipplepen, Devon.
1944–5	Short Naval University Course, Edinburgh.
1945–7	Lieutenant, Royal Marines. Trains recruits at Okehampton Camp, Dartmoor, Devon.
1947–50	Reads Modern Languages at New College, Oxford, specializing in French. Begins writing poetry, philosophical ideas, and a diary, 'Disjoints'.
1950–1	Lecturer in English, University of Poitiers, France.
1951–3	Teacher of English, Anargyrios and Korgialenios School, Spetsai, Greece. Meets Elizabeth Whitton. First published poems written.
1953–4	Teacher of English, Ashridge College, Hertfordshire. Begins writing *The Magus*.
1954	Marries Elizabeth Whitton.
1954–63	Teacher of English, St Godric's College, London.
1960	Begins writing *The Collector*.
1963	*The Collector* published and becomes a best-seller. Leaves his teaching job.
1964	*The Aristos: A Self-Portrait in Ideas* (revised editions 1968 and 1980).
1965	*The Magus* published in USA (first published in UK 1966). Film adaptation of *The Collector*.

1966	John and Elizabeth Fowles move from London to Underhill Farm, near Lyme Regis, Dorset.
1967	Begins writing *The French Lieutenant's Woman*.
1968	The Fowleses move to Belmont House, Lyme Regis. Film adaptation of *The Magus* (screenplay by Fowles).
1969	*The French Lieutenant's Woman* published; wins W. H. Smith & Son Literary Award and PEN Silver Pen Award.
1973	*Poems.*
1974	*The Ebony Tower. Shipwreck*, with photographs by the Gibsons of Scilly.
1977	*Daniel Martin. The Magus: A Revised Version.*
1978	*Islands*, with photographs by Fay Godwin. Appointed joint honorary curator of the Lyme Regis (Philpot) Museum; sole honorary curator 1979–88.
1979	*The Tree*, with photographs by Frank Horvat.
1980	*The Enigma of Stonehenge* (co-author Barry Brukoff).
1981	Film adaptation of *The French Lieutenant's Woman*. Translation of Molière's *Dom Juan* produced by the National Theatre.
1982	*Mantissa.*
1983	Hon. D.Litt., University of Exeter.
1984	Television adaptation of 'The Ebony Tower'.
1985	*A Maggot. Land*, with photographs by Fay Godwin.
1988	Suffers a minor stroke.
1990	Elizabeth Fowles dies of cancer.
1997	Hon. D.Litt., University of East Anglia. Hon. D.Litt., University of Oxford.
1998	*Wormholes: Essays and Occasional Writings*, ed. Jan Relf. Marries Sarah Smith. Hon D.Litt., Chapman University.
1999	*Conversations with John Fowles* (collected interviews), ed. Dianne L. Vipond. Nominated for Nobel Prize for Literature.

Abbreviations and References

A.	*The Aristos*, rev. edn. (London: Triad Grafton, 1981)
C.	*The Collector* (London: Vintage, 1998)
Con.	*Conversations with John Fowles*, ed. Dianne L. Vipond (Jackson: University Press of Mississippi, 1999)
DM	*Daniel Martin* (London: Picador, 1989)
E.	*The Enigma of Stonehenge*, with Barry Brukoff (London: Jonathan Cape, 1980)
ET	*The Ebony Tower* (London: Jonathan Cape, 1974)
FLW	*The French Lieutenant's Woman* (London: Vintage, 1996)
I.	*Islands*, with photographs by Fay Godwin (London: Jonathan Cape, 1978)
LS	'Past and Present Comment: An Afterword', in *Locating the Shakers*, ed. Mick Gidley and Kate Bowles (Exeter: Exeter University Press, 1990), 146–50
M.	*The Magus: A Revised Version* (London: Vintage, 1997)
Mag.	*A Maggot* (London: Jonathan Cape, 1985)
Man.	*Mantissa* (London: Jonathan Cape, 1982)
O.	Claire de Duras, *Ourika, An English Translation*, trans. and foreword by John Fowles (New York: Modern Language Association, 1994)
P.	*Poems* (New York: Ecco Press, 1973)
T.	*The Tree* (London: Vintage, 2000)
UM	unpublished manuscripts (University of Exeter Library)
W.	*Wormholes: Essays and Occasional Writings*, ed. Jan Relf (London: Vintage, 1999)

1

Introduction: The Enigma of John Fowles

In John Fowles's short story 'The Enigma', John Marcus Fielding, an important public figure – Member of Parliament, businessman, farmer, husband, father – suddenly goes missing. He is never found, despite the efforts of the detective assigned to the case. As the characters discuss him, the dialogue becomes a meditation upon storytelling itself: 'Let's pretend everything to do with the Fieldings, even you and me sitting here now, is in a novel. A detective story. Yes? Somewhere there's someone writing us, we're not real. He or she decides who we are, what we do, all about us' (*ET* 229). As this implies, John Fielding is not the only JF under investigation. John Fowles is the 'someone writing us', but, like the vanished politician of 'The Enigma', he is hard to find. He too is a disappearing man, a creator of mysteries. In his novels he offers all sorts of evidence of his presence – narrators who tell us they have written the book, signed prologues, quotations from the documents he has used in his research, sections where he appears to be making the novel up as he goes along, passages spoken by the characters but which seem intended to teach the reader something about life – and yet, none of this is enough to prove beyond reasonable doubt what he really thinks. He takes a significant part in all his stories and yet he cannot be pinned down. He is as elusive as the *deus absconditus*, the god who 'went missing [. . .] without explaining why' (*ET* 235). Like such a god, Fowles creates his fictional universes then has the wisdom (or the cheek) to vanish, leaving his readers to work out what each story means. Instead of an author, Fowles's novels offer personas, or literary masks, which are so complex and varied they hide the real Fowles from his audience. The masks range from Nicholas Urfe, the protagonist of *The Magus* who tells us he is the writer of the novel, to the flashily dressed author-impresario of *The French Lieutenant's Woman*, who is so much part of the characters' world that he even shares a train compartment with the protagonist, to the composer of the Epilogue to *A Maggot*, who declares to the reader that his story does not mimic known history, even though it is full of authentic documents from the eighteenth century reproduced in facsimile.

Fowles knows that even the man discussed by readers, critics, and reviewers is not himself. He has drawn an important distinction between the 'Fowles' of public discourse, 'my representative in the public world, a kind of vulgar waxwork figure' (*W.* 233), and the real Fowles, without the inverted commas, who tends his garden in Lyme Regis. With an irony I hope Fowles will appreciate, this book is intended to leave the gardener largely alone and instead to examine the waxwork figure in all his guises. In keeping with this I have concentrated not on Fowles's personality but on the *idea* of the individual as it applies to the narrators and characters in the novels and the written 'I' of the non-fiction. When reading Fowles's work I have focused on psychology, gender, sexuality, ethnicity, and the other components that make up a person; I have tried to uncover some fresh ways of looking at the texts, in particular by studying the relationship between Fowles's characters and his ideas about identity.

Identity, for Fowles, emerges through conflict. The gradual progress of the individual towards greater autonomy is a key theme of his novels. None of the protagonists (except those of *Mantissa*, who are exceptional cases) is ever the same person at the end of the book as at the beginning; they are always changing as individuals by pursuing their personal goals, or at least attempting to do so, usually in the face of powerful opposition. Nicholas Urfe in *The Magus* tries to make himself worthy of his girlfriend Alison, and to become a writer, despite his own self-centredness; Sarah Woodruff in *The French Lieutenant's Woman* attempts to live outside the morality of society, challenging the overwhelming negative stereotypes affecting independent, sexually active women in Victorian England; Charles Smithson in the same novel ruins his reputation and his marriage prospects by loving Sarah, but may have to start life anew as a single man in America after she abandons him; Rebecca Hocknell in *A Maggot* joins a fringe religious sect, alienating herself from eighteenth-century society.

The protagonists' search for independence is not a simple one. They are all complex, paradoxical beings with faults as well as virtues; Fowles writes not of stereotypes but of developing, growing, organic entities to whom the label 'character' does little justice. He does so because of his philosophy, which has itself evolved organically and is in a constant state of development, but has its roots in existentialism, which he defined as 'the revolt of the individual against all those systems of thought, theories of psychology, and social and political pressures that attempt to rob him of his individuality' (*A*. 115). Existentialism, with its attendant individualism (placing the rights of the one above the demands of the many), is no longer the basis of Fowles's ideas; however, since he began writing seriously in the 1950s, he has continued to explore the complex problem of what it means to be a human being.

In an attempt to reflect Fowles's changing approach to this problem, and in order to document his evolving literary technique, I have divided this book into three sections. Each is devoted to one of the major periods of Fowles's creativity: the early, exploratory phase (1951–65) whose high point was the publication of *The Magus*; the productive middle period of *The French Lieutenant's Woman*, *Daniel Martin*, and a number of other works (1966–79); and the later, highly self-reflexive period from *Mantissa* onwards (1980–2001). This classification is convenient but arbitrary, and is certainly not intended to be prescriptive. I have abandoned it from time to time – *Daniel Martin*, for instance, appears in the chapter on the early work, as well as later on, because its references to 'whole sight' form part of Fowles's philosophy of perception, whose genesis was his early experience of Greece, in particular his ecstatic response to the intensely lit Mediterranean landscape.

Fowles's novels and the ideas within them have changed, but have not 'improved' in any crudely quantifiable way –

consequently, neither the early, the middle, nor the later work should be read as the most significant. I have avoided the temptation to rank his texts, or produce some sort of league table; when writing about Fowles, it is important not to pay too much attention to sorting and classifying, or what he calls *collecting* – the mania for lists and hierarchies, which ultimately cannot cope with a fluid, evolving world. As Fowles has said on more than one occasion when discussing the experience of writing, art is a natural process of selection, discrimination, the subtle evolution of a narrative out of its creator's often confused initial impulse, not a product manufactured according to a formula. He has asked why so little critical attention is devoted to the act of fiction making rather than the fiction itself. This book is intended to go some way towards answering Fowles's plea, by reading his work as an evolving meditation on creativity – from *The Magus*, where the journey of Nicholas Urfe to a Greek island conceals a subtext about the need for the young artist to displace himself from his native culture and seek exile (emotional and intellectual, as well as physical) before his art can properly emerge, to *A Maggot*, a story set in 1736 that refers to real people and events and yet claims to be not a historical novel at all but a mere 'maggot' (meaning whim) of the author.

The theme of creativity is directly connected to my study's other focus, on individual identity. Writing and subjectivity are not, for Fowles, easily separable concepts. To be a writer is to embark on a voyage of self-discovery, as is to be a reader – to think about what it means to be a person, or what it means to write, or what a novel means to you, are closely related activities. This is not meant to imply that Fowles's fictions are dry philosophical tomes thinly disguised as literature. Far from it – as his novels have proved again and again, the reader's voyage of self-discovery can be enjoyable. In *The Magus* Nicholas Urfe has the following conversation with Conchis, the mysterious, all-wise, and forever playful millionaire who is the magus of the title:

> [Conchis] picked up a book and slapped the dust off it. 'Why should I struggle through hundreds of pages of fabrication to reach half a dozen very little truths?'

'For fun?'
'Fun!' He pounced on the word. 'Words are for truth. For facts.
Not fiction.' (*M.* 96)

If Fowles believed this, *The Magus* would not have been a
novel. Conchis, who is a constant teller of lies and weaver of
tales, a fiction-maker in all but name, does not believe it either.
Fowles wants to entertain. He is not ashamed to hold the
reader's attention by using suspense devices and erotic plots
borrowed from popular genres. Unlike most writers of thrillers
or romances, though, Fowles uses fiction to investigate ideas;
he twists old narrative forms into new, beguiling shapes that
allow space for discussion. Like Conchis, who leads the
curious Nicholas into ever stranger situations, Fowles sets up
a range of games to engage the reader, at the same time as
suggesting a few truths as the games progress.

Such truths often arrive in unexpected ways. In 'The
Enigma' the detective protagonist finally gives up his search
for the missing man, having discovered someone far more
interesting – the girlfriend of the man's son. When they finally
become lovers, the narrator takes on the role of *deus absconditus*
and tactfully ends the story, leaving them alone with each
other: 'The tender pragmatisms of flesh have poetries no
enigma, human or divine, can diminish or demean – indeed, it
can only cause them, and then walk out' (*ET* 239).

The 'human' enigma is the vanished John Fielding, who has
unintentionally brought the lovers together. The 'divine' one,
in this context, is John Fowles. There are many such places in
Fowles's work, where he personifies himself as the elusive
creator of a puzzle – a god 'in the new theological image, with
freedom [his] first principle, not authority' (*FLW* 99). His job is
to establish a mystery for the reader, then exit. He does this in
order to allow the reader to become a creative individual – an
artist in his or her own right, rebuilding the world of the text
according to whatever 'pragmatisms' will make it work. In a
1988 interview, he compares reading to writing:

> Reading a novel is an equally creative experience, and the one
> thing the fiction reader does not want to be given is something
> where every question is answered; surely one of the most
> important functions of the novel is to create, not exactly a sense of

mystery, but to leave spaces which the reader has got to fill in.   (*Con.* 155)

Fowles's fictions allow the reader space to think and feel. In the process, he or she learns: first to think about fiction making, nature, psychology, history, or whatever themes taken from Fowles's vast repertoire the text addresses; and, secondly, to respond to his favourite Socratic injunction, know yourself. To this should be added another, typically Fowlesian command: *create* yourself. Beyond all the skill that has crafted their fascinating plots of suspense and desire, what draws such a large audience to Fowles's enigmatic tales is the seductive promise of creativity and self-realization that Conchis offers Nicholas: 'you too now begin to be a magician' (*M.* 552). The author as god of the novel may have disappeared, but in his place comes the questing reader, free to remake the text – and, ultimately, him or herself – in a new image. With this reader, if anywhere, lies the answer to the enigma of John Fowles.

2

Early Period: 1951–1965

> I was born in 1927, the only child of middle-class parents, both
> English, and themselves born in the grotesquely elongated
> shadow, which they never rose sufficiently above history to leave,
> of that monstrous dwarf Queen Victoria. I was sent to a public
> school, I wasted two years doing my national service, I went to
> Oxford; and there I began to discover I was not the person I
> wanted to be. (*M.* 15)

The opening words of *The Magus* are those of the protagonist,
Nicholas Urfe, but they could easily be read as a self-mocking
autobiographical caricature by Fowles. Like Nicholas, Fowles
was brought up in suburbia, went to a public school, then
served in the armed forces (the Marines, whereas Nicholas
joins the Army). By his mid-twenties, he had rejected this
Establishment background, but had formulated no ideology of
his own apart from a vague sense of sympathy with the
existentialism of the French writers he had read as a student at
Oxford from 1947 to 1950. His diary of 6 July 1951 shows that
he was to some extent aware of his partial failure to break
away from his past, and was trying to deal with it:

> I left all that seemed to be expected from a head of school, a Marine
> officer, and started to hack my way out, sideways, to heights I
> couldn't then see for the jungle. All the false tracks, mistakes,
> naivetes, discoveries, resolutions [. . .] but also beginning to see the
> heights. (UM)

Fowles knew he was 'beginning to see the heights' of the
creative freedom and existential authenticity that he so keenly
sought, but was at the same time still restricted by his
self-confessed 'naivetes'. His immaturity was literary as well as

personal. In the 1950s, when he was trying to compose the early drafts of *The Magus*, his first attempt at long fiction, 'Both technique and that bizarre face of the imagination that seems to be more like a failure to remember the already existent than what it really is – a failure to evoke the non-existent – kept me miserably aground' (*M*. 5).

Fortunately, despite Fowles's initial failures of imagination, *The Magus* finally appeared in 1965. The novel, with its strong narrative sustained through all the fantastical twists and turns of the plot, shows that Fowles was in the end able to rework his early drafts successfully. Like Nicholas Urfe, he was hired under the auspices of the British Council to teach English as a foreign language at a boys' boarding school on a Greek island (Spetsai, which become Phraxos in the novel); Fowles stayed there from 1951 to 1953. He turned his experience of the island into a carnivalesque *tour de force*, which, whether loved or hated by its readers, is rarely forgotten. The plot of the novel is far too complex to summarize adequately, but its key mechanism, the meta-theatre, can be explained briefly. Nicholas's work as a teacher begins predictably enough, but he soon meets the mysterious millionaire Maurice Conchis, who invites him to his isolated villa, Bourani, where stranger and stranger events occur around him; he seems to have walked into a waking dream or never-ending masque. Conchis's own image for the events at Bourani is that of a new kind of theatre, without any firm distinction between the script and real life, where 'the conventional separation between actors and audience [is] abolished' (*M*. 404) and which can ultimately encompass the whole world: 'There is no place for limits in the meta-theatre' (*M*. 406). Nicholas is beset by puzzles, traps, strange scenes in the moonlight, intellectual and sexual games played by a cast whose roles and personalities seem forever to be shifting. Consequently he is unable to acquire any firm grasp of his relationship to those around him. Eventually even his sense of his own identity, so certain at the start of the novel (and exemplified in the arrogant self-portrait quoted at the beginning of this chapter), begins to weaken. Conchis reinforces this in a speech that includes Nicholas among the cast of the meta-theatre: 'We are all actors here, my friend. None of us is what we really are. We all lie some of the time, and some of us all the time' (*M*. 404).

Despite the duplicitous complexity of Conchis's games, Nicholas retains a touching faith in his own attractiveness to the opposite sex. He meets two Englishwomen at Bourani, twin sisters of about his own age, conceives a passion for one of them and imagines that it is requited. The sisters have no fixed identity: sometimes they are Lily and Rose, sometimes Julie and June; sometimes they claim to Nicholas that they are actresses hired by Conchis, sometimes they seem to be sincere. Nicholas's love for Lily grows despite his attachment to his girlfriend Alison, an air hostess whom he has left behind in London. Alison flies to Athens and the couple are reunited, but Nicholas breaks the news to her about Lily. After that, he returns to the island. He later hears that Alison has committed suicide, but in a devastating narrative reversal, discovers that this is a lie concocted by Conchis, and that Alison is alive and waiting for the moment when he will have achieved sufficient personal growth to be worthy of her. She too has joined Conchis's drama, which has extended beyond Bourani to encompass the world. The meta-theatre has revealed its purpose – to educate Nicholas in a way that is still not fully comprehensible to him, despite the many hints given by Conchis, such as: 'The object of the meta-theatre is [. . .] to allow the participants to see through their first roles in it' and thus 'to see through the roles we give ourselves in ordinary life' (*M.* 408–9). Nicholas eventually returns to London and meets Alison again. He believes that they have left Conchis's drama behind them, though it remains uncertain whether they have a future together.

By the end of the novel, Nicholas is finally becoming a worthy pupil of Conchis. He is beginning to evolve into an authentic individual, able to write his own destiny, critically examining the roles he and Alison have allotted themselves in life, having begun his time on the island as the mere *tabula rasa* on which the old millionaire and his minions wrote the script of their bizarre existentialist masque. Nicholas evolves not only personally, but as an artist. Before meeting Conchis, he decides he has no future as a poet and, in a moment of typically overwrought self-pity, decides to kill himself with a shotgun. He abandons the attempt at the crucial moment. Immediately afterwards the novel shifts to a narrative future, 'Years later'

9

(*M.* 62), well after Nicholas's experience on the island. Writing from this future he is able with hindsight to see his juvenile poetry and aborted suicide as the same thing, 'attempts at escape' (*M.* 63). Nicholas is now a prose writer, composing *The Magus* itself. He adopts the retrospective viewpoint of an autobiographer writing his memoirs, coupled with a distinctly Fowlesian tone of self-criticism, as if reviewing his own struggle towards the authentic selfhood he would eventually achieve. As Fowles said in an interview in 1985:

> [Nicholas] *is* writing his own story – and no critic has ever taken that into account. All these terrible things they say about him – that he's a typical, totally selfish, modern man – they've never noticed that he's saying these things about himself. He's talking about 'as he was' from a present (of which you know nothing) to a past. (*Con.* 120)

Nicholas looks back to his own past in *The Magus* – and likewise, in the interview, Fowles is looking back on *his* own past, reflecting upon the misguided critical reception of his own handling of Nicholas in the novel. In defending Nicholas, he is also justifying the autobiographical frame of the narrative that he believes critics failed to notice.

In a sense, both Fowles *and* Nicholas wrote *The Magus*. The novel, when read as the story of the formation of Nicholas as a novelist, comes to seem like a self-reflexive narrative about the intellectual and emotional journey of Fowles as a young would-be writer, which knowingly blurs the identities of author and character. *The Magus* is far too fantastical to be Fowles's autobiography; nevertheless, it is his definitive early text. It functions as a life story on a symbolic level, forming an elaborate pattern of 'metaphorical descriptions of complex modes of feeling' (*M.* 17) including Fowles's own emotions about his youthful attempts at creativity. Also underlying the story, with its elusive, desirable heroines, was Fowles's own temporary separation from his future wife, Elizabeth Whitton, whom he had met on Spetsai. Elizabeth was at that time married to another teacher. When Fowles began to compose *The Magus*, she had returned to England but was still with her then husband: an 'unresolved sense of a lack, a missed opportunity, led me to graft certain dilemmas of a private situation in England on the memory of the island and its solitudes' (*M*. 9). The text signifies Elizabeth's powerful influence in another, subtler way, through its demonstration of the inspirational effect Conchis has on the young man; Fowles later regretted that he had not made Conchis a woman (*W*. 26). The old millionaire is, in a sense, a male muse, the provider of the imaginative resources lacked by Nicholas, the aspirant writer. Elizabeth herself, as Fowles would later confess, was his real-life equivalent of a muse; her ghost lay behind all the heroines in his fiction (*Con*. 196). Clearly, Nicholas's quest for sexual and artistic fulfilment closely paralleled that of his creator.

At the same time, though, Nicholas's quest gave Fowles an opportunity to explore wider themes – in particular, that of the individual's proper relationship to his or her environment, meaning not only landscape but also culture. At a key moment in the novel, Nicholas and Alison climb Mount Parnassus, home of the Muses, and find that someone has left there the word *phos*, written with stones. 'It was exact. The peak reached up into a world both literally and metaphorically of light'; the view from the summit gives Nicholas 'a delicious intellectual joy marrying and completing the physical one' (*M*. 258). The primary quality of living in Greece was, for Fowles, *phos* or light – a word that has multiple resonances in his work, both in the original Greek and in English. In his 1994 essay 'Behind *The Magus*', Fowles revealed that he saw the same view himself, and the same word, also written with stones, surrounded by a ring of violets, on the top of Parnassus in 1953. He said that it took him over thirty years to understand the true impact of light in the Greek sense, when he came to understand that *phos* 'is all beauty and all truth. [. . .] It and its absence are life and death' (*W*. 76).

Despite the enormous significance of *phos* to Fowles, defining it is difficult. *Phos* is a medium by which the world is viewed, but it also transforms the viewer from outside, *creating* him or her, and revitalizing his or her relationship to the world, rather than merely representing it. Although according to Fowles *phos* is the normal medium of vision for the Greek people in their native land – they 'apprehend light not as others do' (*W*. 75) – it is by no means accessible to the non-Greek eye reared on package tours. Here, the concept

11

begins to look problematic; it is geographically and ethnically specific, although potentially available to foreigners, especially relatively cultured ones like Nicholas. I do not mean to undermine Fowles's idea, but to qualify it by showing how it is dependent upon a sense of national identity. Not all nations were as privileged as the Greeks; indeed, Fowles believed that *phos* was specifically alien to the English. In one of his earliest essays, 'On Being English but not British' (*W*. 91–103), Fowles constructed Englishness as concealment; as a Robin Hood-like spirit of rebellion, hiding in the forest from the rule of the Sheriff of Nottingham (representing, in Fowles's modern interpretation of the medieval English legend, the power of the British state, which was an artificially imposed mechanism designed to govern four separate peoples, the English, Irish, Scots, and Welsh). Fowles implied that the natural medium of the English was darkness, the opposite of *phos*. To be English was to be able knowingly to withdraw into mental shadows: 'a harried "free" man, a Robin Hood in each, retreats into the forests of the private mind' (*A*. 39).

Fowles, in his early fictions, especially *The Magus*, was seeking to free himself from his own English retreat into the shadows of the psyche by means of an ongoing experiment with words and concepts. His aim was to view himself, and his relationship to the world, with a clear vision, untrammelled by received ideas. *Phos* is an early incarnation of this ambition. It is still present, in an evolved form, in his later work; his 1977 novel *Daniel Martin* begins with the words, 'Whole sight; or all the rest is desolation' (*DM* 7). The eponymous protagonist, a screenwriter and would-be novelist, places great importance on perception:

> He was too English, of course, to take Zen very seriously as a philosophy, but it had strengthened in him a feeling that some inner truth lay in the perception of the transient. He would have been embarrassed to define and justify it, but it lay somewhere in the importance of presentness in life; just as the value he attached to it was betrayed by his demanding or expecting more of the present than it was usually prepared to give. (*DM* 612–13)

Here, 'inner truth' is brought to Daniel by his English adaptation of an Eastern philosophy, Zen Buddhism, to his own needs. Again, insight is mediated by ethnicity (Daniel's nationality is crucial to his interpretation of Zen), but Fowles's term for an existentially authentic vision of the self and the world has shifted from *phos* – a quality inherent in certain privileged environments, which has the power to transform the viewer – to whole sight, a way of seeing the environment that comes from *within* the viewer, and is cultivated through the study of philosophy as much as through actual seeing.

Fowles's decision to construct both *phos* and whole sight in terms of the encounter of an Englishman with a foreign environment or idea is far from coincidental. Fowles was, and is, a consummate member of his post-imperial generation; he grew into artistic maturity within a nation still living inside the image of its former colonial dominance, but nevertheless struggling to renegotiate its place in the world by embracing intellectual and emotional, as well as literal, foreign travel. In 1964 he wrote, 'This greenness [of England] is not very fashionable at the moment; it is the burned rock of the south that we long for, and more than that for the burned, black, cynical experience of mainland Europe' (*W*. 102).

The Magus plays ironically with Fowles's generation's quest for the wisdom of other cultures. Fowles himself knew its limitations, having had personal experience of the extent to which the English traveller abroad in the 1950s might find only England reproduced or unconsciously parodied. On Spetsai, he found himself working in the Anargyrios and Korgialenios School, an institution that explicitly modelled itself on the English national myth of the great 'public' (actually private, fee-paying) school, supposedly the mould of a robust but fair-minded and honourable national character. Fowles, with his boyhood experience of Bedford School, where he rose to become head boy (that is, chief pupil, one of whose duties was flogging transgressors), had a highly sceptical understanding of that myth, and by extension the concept of an eminently worthy Englishness that ought to be copied by foreigners:

> to be immured in what was apparently an absurd simulacrum of a British private school, was ridiculous [. . .] I had once been head boy of my own outwardly not dissimilar school in England (Bedford), but it had taken Oxford, existentialism mingled with the

13

siren voices of Marxism, and several intervening years (they call it growing up) for me at last shamefacedly to reject all the shoddy little triumphs of my personal past. (*W*. 80)

He sought and found *phos* outside his own native society, whose microcosm was the public school in England and its imitation in Greece. In order to do so, he staked his philosophical capital 'on two outsiders: "Europe" and "woman" ' (*W*. 85); the incarnations of these in *The Magus* are the pan-European, cosmopolitan Conchis and Alison, who is not British but Australian.

Fowles's early intellectual investment in feminism and foreignness was underwritten by the search for the Other – whatever is not-Self, the outsider. Most of Fowles's protagonists are seekers, who try to develop themselves through encounters with other people, or, more usually, one other important person, generally of another gender, ethnic group, and/or social class. *The Magus* establishes a recurring theme that is played out with a number of variations throughout all of Fowles's fictions – the dualism of magus and initiate. The magus is the wiser, often older character who guides the initiate in his or her search for knowledge and personal growth. The usual setting for their educative dialogue is not a classroom or other public place, but what Fowles calls the *domaine*, a private space whose literary origin lies in medieval romance, but which has had many later incarnations, most significantly for Fowles in Henri Alain-Fournier's *Le Grand Meaulnes*, a novel 'which has had an extraordinary emotional effect on me all my life' (*Con*. 88). The *domaine* is an enclosure of mystery and romance, set apart from normal life, in which the initiate frequently comes to discover that the 'reality' he or she has left behind is in fact the illusion, and that the *domaine* can awaken and transform his or her sense of identity. Nicholas, finally realizing that other visitors to Bourani have experienced Conchis's games before, and that the old man and his associates are deliberately performing roles for him, and the meta-theatre has a purpose he as yet does not understand, self-consciously writes himself into a romance: 'I had entered the domaine' (*M*. 134). The *domaine* is a magical place, with the power to transmute reality; for Nicholas, it was 'As if the world had suddenly, during those last three days, been re-invented, and for me alone' (*M.* 157).

Nicholas's words give a clue to Fowles's view of the creative process as the construction of a highly personal world – a *domaine* within the mind of the writer. Fowles has claimed that one of the main pleasures of composition is that it educates and changes the composer, so both artist and artefact evolve at the same time: 'the person who always benefits and learns most from the maze, the voyage, the mysterious island [i.e. the evolving text], is the inventor, the traveller, the visitor . . . that is, the artist-artificer himself' (*I.* 98; ellipsis in original). The creative act is solipsistic and yet spiritual, sacred and yet ludic (driven by what Fowles calls *keraunos*, or hazard). Fowles's term for the process of composition, combining all these associations, was also the original subtitle of *The Magus*: The Godgame. Creativity is analogous to God's creation of the universe; in Fowles's philosophy, God, like a novelist, disappears once he has created his text (the universe) and leaves his readers (humanity) to work out what is going on, or whether He even exists. Fowles has always maintained that he is not an atheist, but is forced to act in all public matters as if he is one, presumably because of the absence of any verifiable deity. If a god existed, he would have had to efface himself: 'Put dice on the table and leave the room; but make it seem possible to the players that you were never in the room' (*A.* 18–19). Dice imply an aleatory contest, or gamble. God's having determined natural laws, but leaving the rest to hazard, is the reason for Fowles's choice of the noun god*game*. The departure of the *deus absconditus* is seen as a major source of motivation for the human players of the game: 'Mystery, or unknowing, is energy [. . .] since 'God' is unknowable, we cannot dam the spring of basic existential mystery' (*A.* 27). Fowles's novels draw from the energy source of this mystery, and narrate the individual's quest to make sense of it. This quest is usually frustrating and lengthy, reaching no definitive conclusion. In his 1974 essay on Conan Doyle, Fowles places great importance on the *absence* of any conclusion to the quest, as should a mystery be solved, its power disappears. 'However fantastic and far-reaching the first half of a detective "mystery", the second half is bound to drop (and only too often flop) towards a neat and plausible everyday solution' (*W.* 157).

15

To Fowles, the detective story in its traditional form fails to recognize the complexity of the world; the mystery of existence cannot be solved because the universe is not a fixed, determinate structure. The point of the mystery is not the solution, but the act of working to solve it. In *Islands*, Fowles points out that there was a guide to the famous maze at Hampton Court that showed visitors the shortest route to the middle: 'Nobody who used it ever reached the centre; which lies not in the unravelled, but the unravelling' (*I*. 106). Wandering in the maze is a metaphor not only for reading, but also for writing, and the labyrinth is a symbol of the author's creativity: 'The maze is also a very ancient symbol of ingenuity in craftsmanship, of the ability to fabricate, to sew and weave beyond ordinary skill – in other words, it is the prime proof of the artificer, or artist' (*I*. 93).

The Magus is a novel about labyrinths. Nicholas frequently uses the metaphor of a maze to describe his experience. Attempting to interpret the mysteries Conchis sets before him, he sees himself as Theseus trapped in 'a legendary maze' with Lily as his Ariadne (*M*. 210). It is even equipped with a 'Minotaur' (*M*. 313) in a threatening ethnic Other, the black American actor Joe Harrison, who turns out to be Lily's lover. Later on, Nicholas sees Conchis's labyrinth as a laboratory maze with rats overseen by a scientist (*M*. 404), then finally, Nicholas realizes 'the maze has no centre. An ending is no more than a point in sequence, a snip of the cutting shears' (*M*. 645). Fowles alludes both to the process of cutting a film for the cinema and to the fatal cut of the thread of a person's life made by the three Fates of Greek mythology. Thus both modern artistic technologies and ancient deterministic myths (fate) are made to become part of a greater maze, the world itself. The labyrinth-as-reality is endless as well as centreless; any humanly constructed ending is arbitrary, and on a higher meta-human level is no ending at all. The earliest type of maze cited by Nicholas, the legendary one negotiated by Theseus, is derived from classical sources; it has a clear goal (the princess as a prize), a defined enemy (the Minotaur), and an escape route (Ariadne's thread); the second type of labyrinth Nicholas mentions, the laboratory maze, is a product of Enlightenment empiricism, controlled by an all-powerful but ultimately knowable and rational subject, the scientist; both these types of labyrinth are superseded by the postmodern version, the maze that has 'no centre' because it is a metaphor for reality – an unknowable, endless, ever-changing pattern without a mythical or rational centre to control it. The labyrinth in its final incarnation is what the philosophers Gilles Deleuze and Félix Guattari would call a rhizome, a potentially endless system with no fixed points of entry or exit: 'an acentred, nonhierarchical, nonsignifying system without a General and without an organizing memory or central automaton, defined solely by a circulation of states.'[1] The contemporary novelist and semiotician Umberto Eco uses their terminology to describe *The Name of the Rose*, his own well-known novel of labyrinths; its world 'has a rhizome structure: that is, it can be structured but is never structured definitively'.[2] Similarly, *The Magus* is a rhizome; its ending is not a final solution to Nicholas's dilemmas, its many episodes are interconnected but no single one is dominant, and the novel as a whole resists any simple interpretation. Fowles has insisted that 'Its meaning is whatever reaction it provokes in the reader, and so far as I am concerned there is no given "right" reaction' (*M*. 9).

In the 1950s and early 1960s Fowles was an inexperienced writer attempting a novel with an enormously complex rhizomatic architecture. To Fowles, at least, the result was a partial failure. In 1977, in an attempt to remove a few of what he thought were its most remediable faults, he published *The Magus: A Revised Version*, the text which is in print today (and which I have cited in this book). In his foreword to the new edition, Fowles argued that *The Magus* was 'a novel of adolescence written by a retarded adolescent' (*M*. 9). It was, as he saw with hindsight, a variation on *Le Grand Meaulnes*, but, whereas Alain-Fournier's novel narrated the frustrated longings of an 'open and specific' adolescence (*M*. 6), *The Magus* concealed its own callowness in a failed quest for literary maturity. Fowles was perhaps too harsh a judge of his own early work; nevertheless, the fact that he bothered to revise his own novel twelve years after first publication shows that the exploratory self-consciousness of his early phase was maintained in later periods. Indeed, he has never abandoned his belief that creativity is a process of personal growth, of

17

perpetual self-revision, rather than the factory-like production of a series of texts on demand. In 1984, in his foreword to H. W. Fawkner's study *The Timescapes of John Fowles*, he remarked:

> I write fiction very much to discover myself through texts – more precisely during the process of writing them – and very little to stake a claim on the flagrant quicksand of contemporary reputation. [. . .] My fictions are far more experiments than anything else – that is, in search of something, or things, always beyond the outward narrative and themes. This is a main reason why I find that writing, except on one or two superficial technical levels, does not get easier as I grow older; and why I have changed direction so often in the past, in orthodox literary terms.[3]

This passage exemplifies Fowles's ambivalent acceptance of the paradoxical mixture of change and consistency that he finds within the creative process. As an artist, he is forever creating new textual apparatuses (usually, but not always, novels) to experiment with ideas, but is doing so according to certain more or less consistent principles, most notably that of self-discovery. *The Magus*, with its tortuous genesis and eventual success, was the place where Fowles first put this principle into practice: 'The Magus remained essentially where a tyro taught himself to write novels – beneath its narrative, a notebook of an exploration, often erring and misconceived, into an unknown land' (*M.* 5).

The Magus is a novel of adolescence, but Fowles also places great importance on the writer's infancy: 'A novelist must cherish all his ages, perhaps his child self most of all; the cost is that he will always be in exile from his society, above all from the society of his contemporaries. Most of mine seem increasingly older than I am to me, in every ordinary social and cultural sense'.[4] In his view, ageing and literary development are not simple linear processes but are organic, subjective, and psychologically structured – a matter of self-perception, or how old 'I am to me' – in a way alien to calendars, clocks, and the genealogical conventions of literary criticism.

It seems fitting, then, that Fowles's early period does not offer the reader a straightforward, easily traceable pattern of artistic evolution. His first published novel, *The Collector*, was begun in 1960, a long time after his first attempts at *The Magus*. It was born of Fowles's personal frustration at his lack of success, his self-conscious wish to explore genres, and his pragmatic knowledge of the workings of the market. In the early 1960s, *The Magus* had been substantially written and several times revised, but Fowles was approaching 40 years of age, and was still unpublished. Uncertain of whether he would ever have a career as a writer, he set out to prove the case one way or the other, by writing the most commercial novel he could manage without sacrificing his commitment to ideas. Seeking a story, he attended a performance of Bela Bartók's opera *Bluebeard's Castle*, in which the protagonist captures women: 'It wasn't a very good performance, but the thing that struck me was the symbolism of the man imprisoning women underground' (*Con.* 2). This, along with 'a bizarre real-life incident in the 1950s' in which a man shut a woman up in an air-raid shelter (*W.* 173) gave him the raw material he needed. The result was his most immediately accessible work. *The Collector* fascinated (and still fascinates) readers on many psychological and intellectual levels, but the text was re-viewed, in Britain at least, mostly as a straightforward thriller, a reductive categorization of the novel that irritated Fowles at the time (*Con.* 21). The British reviewers' mistake was under-standable, as *The Collector*'s plot conforms to the genre; Miranda Grey, a young art student, is kidnapped by a clerk, Frederick Clegg, who has become obsessed with her. The novel begins with his account of observing and following her, driven by a compulsion to watch and be near her (he 'stalks' her, in the contemporary English idiom). It then shifts to Miranda's diary, kept while he holds her prisoner in his cellar, then returns, for a short but unforgettably sinister coda, to Clegg's narrative, where he buries Miranda, who has died of what seems to be pneumonia. The novel's style is very different from that of *The Magus*; Clegg's halting, crude narration and Miranda's more fluent but callow discourse contrast strongly with the philosophical perorations of Conchis, for example. *The Collector* functions very effectively as a thriller, but it also relies on a much older literary convention; it derives from romance tales of enclosure in confined spaces (Clegg and Miranda

19

resemble a monster and a princess in an updated dungeon). The theme of captivity is encapsulated in the novel's three-part structure; the two sections of Clegg's first-person narrative enclose the middle section, Miranda's diary, just like the walls of the basement that entrap her.

Although the reception of *The Collector* as a thriller annoyed Fowles, he knew that the genre had considerable resources; it offered him space for social critique as well as commercial success. In his essay on Conan Doyle he argued that the thriller evolved from the detective story because, as well as avoiding the banality of narrating the legal process, the genre allowed the author's intellectual and social concerns to be expressed in a form attractive to readers. By writing a thriller, 'a Chandler can criticize right-wing America, a Le Carré can explore the psychology of deception, in a way that the cramping demands of the old crime-solution formula do not allow' (*W*. 157). In *The Collector*, Fowles adopted the methods of these popular writers. He adeptly concealed a social 'parable' (*A*. 10) beneath a story of a kidnapper and his victim. The conflict between the two protagonists was intended to represent the struggle of the Few and the Many, two terms Fowles adapted from the Greek philosopher Heracleitus to refer to the minority tendency in human society towards insight, altruism, generosity, and creativity, and to the majority tendency to blindness, greed, self-ignorance, and creative barrenness. Fowles has never believed that the Few and the Many are two definable social groups; to do so would lead to Fascism, the idea that the Few ought to rule absolutely, regardless of the wishes of the Many, because they are best equipped to do so. Instead, in a crucial qualification of his idea, Fowles argues that '*the dividing line between the Few and the Many must run through each individual, not between individuals*' (*A*. 9; emphasis in original). The interaction between Clegg and Miranda demonstrates how tortuous and hard to trace the dividing line really is. Clegg is an inarticulate clerical worker; Miranda seems, on the surface, to be his exact opposite. She is middle-class, educated, beautiful, intelligent, and talented. However, after Clegg has seized her and locked her in his cellar, the text works out the disturbing connections between them, eroding their differences. Shyamal Bagchee has pointed out that both characters believe in a non-existent or uncaring god, both despise the arrogance of ex-public schoolboys (as Fowles did when repudiating his own background), and both stand out from ordinary members of their social class.[5] In Miranda's words, 'It's weird. Uncanny. But there is a sort of relationship between us' (C. 139); she even compares them, in their familiarity with one another, to 'two people who've been married years' (C. 140).

Miranda's image is a perceptive one. She and Clegg create a secret home within a home together. Locked in the basement beneath his house, she reads, draws, and listens to her favourite records; and, in an ironic inversion of gender roles, Clegg does the cooking and other domestic chores (he even cleans Miranda's lavatory). Perhaps the most worrying implication of this for Fowles's audience – which, despite feminism, arguably applies as much today as in 1963 – is not Clegg's kidnapping of Miranda at all, but their relationship's reproduction, in grotesque and sometimes inverted form, of the conventions of bourgeois domesticity. Clegg's cellar represents the dark Other side of the suburban living room; like the Victorian sensation novels of such writers as Wilkie Collins and Mary Elizabeth Braddon, Fowles's narrative moves the horror away from the Gothic castle and towards the supposedly safe atmosphere of home. The cellar is homely and unhomely at the same time – or, in Sigmund Freud's terms, both *heimlich* and *unheimlich* (uncanny). In 'The Uncanny', his essay on horror stories, Freud argued that we are disturbed when the familiar world of home and everyday life is shown to carry within it a concealed realm of horrible secrets. The essay explores the old Gothic theme of the double (whose classic example in English literature is Mary Shelley's *Frankenstein*, in which the monster created by the eponymous scientist comes to haunt him and follow him everywhere). One aspect of doubling is 'the constant recurrence of the same thing – the repetition of the same features or character-traits or vicissitudes, of the same crimes, or even the same names through several consecutive generations'.[6] If Clegg's cellar is an uncanny *space*, doubling the domestic interior of the bourgeois reader, the novel is also structured with an uncanny sense of *time*. At the end of his narrative, Clegg thinks about repeating his crime. Almost without realizing what he is doing, he plans to kidnap another woman:

> I have not made up my mind about Marian (another M! I heard the supervisor call her name), this time it won't be love, it would just be for the interest of the thing and to compare them and also the other thing, which as I say I would like to go into in more detail and I could teach her how. And the clothes would fit. Of course I would make it clear from the start who's boss and what I expect. (C. 283)

This is a deliberate refusal of narrative closure, offering the reader the sense of mystery that Fowles believes fiction should preserve, and, at the same time, threatening to start the novel all over again. Had Clegg repented and led a law-abiding life, or committed suicide beside Miranda, as he had originally planned to do, the novel would have been ruined by bathos. Instead, he is compelled to repeat his crime, *but the text does not narrate his doing so*. Clegg's second crime remains mysterious, unspoken; in one of the oldest devices of horror stories, the abominable act is left to the reader's imagination. Clegg's planned repetition of the kidnapping, and the similarities of the new victim to the old, are certainly uncanny in Freud's sense: 'For a moment it gave me a turn, I thought I was seeing a ghost' (C. 281).

In seeking the ghost of Miranda, compelled to stalk an M who looks just like the M he has lost, Clegg echoes not only Freud's essay, but also Fowles's own ideas about the deep-rooted psychic impulse underlying the creative process. Some years after writing *The Collector*, Fowles read an article on his fiction by the American psychiatrist Gilbert J. Rose.[7] In the essay 'Hardy and the Hag' (1977), Fowles develops Rose's argument that the male novelist is driven by a compulsion to seek an idealized female figure who stands for his mother as she existed to him in the time of early infancy, before the onset of the Oedipus complex. When the novelist creates his main women characters, he must ensure that their relationships with the male protagonist are either unconsummated or at least never develop into any lasting union. He continues searching for the mother through the medium of fiction; the protagonist's recurring, perpetually frustrated desire for the heroine is the source of the novel's narrative drive. The key factor is *loss* – the novelist creates out of his constant desire to find a goal that will always elude him. Fowles's chief example is Thomas Hardy's late and little-known novel *The Well-Beloved*. Fowles uses its title as his term for the idealized mother figure that the male novelist seeks. In Hardy's novel, the protagonist, a male artist, forms attachments to three different generations of women called Avice. This fits Freud's pattern of doubling perfectly ('the same names through several consecutive generations'), but Avice remains perpetually elusive – Hardy's hero seeks the same woman in all, and never finds her. Clegg, with his compulsive stalking of M-women, is thus the most unlikely incarnation of the novelist in Fowles's *œuvre*. It is, of course, highly improbable that Fowles considered Clegg in this light when composing the novel, but nevertheless the names Miranda and Marian may well have had a subconscious significance for Fowles (as well as being obvious allusions to *The Tempest* and the Robin Hood legend). He later came to realize that, like Clegg, he is M(other)-fixated. In a 1995 interview Dianne L. Vipond pointed out the recurrence of the letters MA in the titles of all his novels (except, strangely, *The Collector*). He conceded that 'Writers are often blind to clues like this about their work. It had never occurred to me before. But yes, I see I am indeed M-dominated. Perhaps in part through my attachment to feminism' (*W.* 440). Such a coincidence of titles may seem trivial, but Vipond asked about it, and Fowles chose to respond, out of an awareness of the significance of patterns of repetition and psycho-sexual compulsion in his work.

This psychological interpretation need not conflict with Fowles's own account of a parable of the Many and the Few. Part of the novel's strength is that it allows room for sociological and psychoanalytical readings, with the confined space of Clegg's cellar ironically acting as a wide, fertile territory for critical exploration. It is a tribute to the economy of *The Collector* that such a range of interpretation is possible. By avoiding the intellectual games of Fowles's other novels (Conchis's ambiguous speeches about existentialism, the pseudo-academic footnotes of *The French Lieutenant's Woman*, the play with cinematic technique in *Daniel Martin*, for example) *The Collector* fails to reach their level of overt cleverness, but is thus free to offer a concise, compelling imitation of a popular genre that conceals its thematic complexity beneath the straightforwardness of its plot. The reader knows in detail what Clegg and Miranda do and say, and turns the pages in response to the novel's successful range of suspense devices, but is offered little evidence of *why* it is all happening, apart from the frustrated speculations of Miranda. That may be precisely because the novel is a device to make the reader think – to force him or her to examine the power games and rituals that underlie routine existence. When Miranda resignedly writes, 'I never see anyone else. He becomes the norm. I forget to compare' (*C.* 189), the text implicitly requires the reader to do the comparing for her, and examine just how near Clegg *is* to the 'norm' of socially acceptable masculinity, and just how many stones from Blue-beard's castle are built into the foundations of the ordinary suburban home.

The Collector is not as far from *The Magus* as it might first seem. Both texts share a subtext of observation and coercion; both are narratives of snooping, of the overt and subtle exercise of power, the manipulation of other people's minds and bodies. Here, I wish to connect the two novels, by considering how power operates within and between them. This can best be done by reading them through the theories of Michel Foucault, who discussed power relations in his seminal account of the origins of the prison, *Discipline and Punish*. Foucault argued that prison architecture and the practices of disciplining and monitoring inmates did not arise by accident. Instead, he examined their evolution in the eighteenth and nineteenth centuries, using a number of central concepts: power, panopticism, discipline. Foucault, discussing 'the Benthamite physics of power', concludes:

> There are two images, then, of discipline. At one extreme, the discipline-blockade, the enclosed institution, established on the edges of society, turned inwards towards negative functions: arresting evil, breaking communications, suspending time. At the other extreme, with panopticism, is the discipline-mechanism: a

functional mechanism that must improve the exercise of power by making it lighter, more rapid, more effective, a design of subtle coercion for a society to come.[8]

Foucault refers first to isolated institutions such as the prison and the madhouse, and then to panopticism. The term comes from Jeremy Bentham's design for the *Panopticon*, a prison arranged so that all cells could be seen by the warders all the time; the prisoners are unaware whether they are being watched, but are under the constant threat of surveillance. On a wider societal level, panopticism is the regulatory regime that ensures that order is maintained because all citizens are observed, or are persuaded to behave *as if* they are observed, the whole time. Without being sidetracked into a detailed discussion of the complex ideas of *Discipline and Punish*, I want to argue that Fowles's early fictions neatly bring together the two 'extremes' of discipline described by Foucault. The playful, creative *domaine* of Conchis's villa at Bourani, and its opposite, the stifling enclosure of Clegg's cellar, are both isolated spaces – institutions of a sort, with a traditional symbolic architecture derived from medieval romance and Gothic fantasy – that exist 'on the edges of society' and that, either through persuasion or through force, compel their inmates to remain. At the same time, *The Collector* and *The Magus* subtly echo the patterns of surveillance found in Foucault's account of Benthamite panopticism. Nicholas, even in some of his most intimate moments (such as the ascent of Parnassus with Alison, and his making love to her there), is being watched, and often filmed, by Conchis's employees. Clegg and Miranda are constantly observing one another and recording their observations in their narratives. Both have moments alone, but the novel comes to life when they record their existence *together*, eye to eye.

The Foucauldian subtext of observation and coercion shared by *The Collector* and *The Magus* is closely connected to Fowles's early fascination with existentialism, and at the same time renders it problematic. As a student, he 'read all of Camus, most of Sartre' (*Con.* 88); these and other French thinkers had persuaded the young Fowles that it is the responsibility of each person, through his or her own actions, to create an authentic mode of individual existence. His novels, however, show how proto-authentic individuals such as Miranda and Nicholas Urfe develop through being watched and trapped, disciplined and punished, by others. (Foucault's title in the original French was *Surveiller et punir* – the first verb means both 'to watch' and 'to regulate', hence the translation 'discipline'.) Fowles was evidently too self-critical and too astute, too unlike the arrogant Nicholas Urfe of *The Magus*'s opening pages, to create novels of simple, linear personal development, in which other characters are mere obstacles to, or distractions from, the protagonists' ultimately attained goals. Instead, his early fictions critically examine, as well as celebrate, his existentialist credo. They ask questions such as: how does one person's inner growth manifest itself outwardly? How will it affect others? Does the individual seeking self-fulfilment sometimes conclude that this cannot, in fact, be reached alone? The latter is true of Nicholas, who, just at the moment when he decides that he has escaped Conchis's panopticism, because he and Alison are no longer observed, or within the rules of the old man's godgame, realizes that he will 'never be more than half a human being' without her (*M*. 655). It is also true, though with horrible irony, of Miranda, who matures significantly when her imprisonment by Clegg forces her to come to terms with the inadequacies of her earlier world view.

Both *The Magus* and *The Collector* are studies of the relationship between subjective development and intersubjective power relations – or, put another way, between authenticity and authority. It is difficult to buy the first without paying the price of imposing, or submitting to, the second. The novels' power structures demonstrate the dialectical relationship of the two. It is as if, in striving to demonstrate a Sartrean philosophy of individual liberty, Fowles's texts expose the dependency of this goal on the Benthamite architecture of power discussed by Foucault. (Or, as Jacques Lacan, the French psychoanalyst, pithily put it in 1949, existentialism offers 'a freedom that is never more authentic than when it is within the walls of a prison'.[9]) Fowles was aware of this problem; in *The Aristos*, the collection of philosophical *pensées* (short thoughts) he published after *The Collector*, he conceded that 'existentialism is conspicuously unsuited to political or social subversion, since it is incapable of organized dogmatic resistance' (*A.* 117). He added that the existentialist can only resist alone, through acts such as *The Aristos* itself. The difficulty with this is the same one that his novels expose – the would-be existentialist individual may be defined *as* an individual by the power relations he or she seeks to resist, in particular, his or her relationships with dominant others such as the magus figure. In another section of *The Aristos*, Fowles theorizes about what he calls 'countersupporting' or the mutual dependency of opposite tendencies upon one another for energy (*A.* 69–72). The relationship of Clegg and Miranda, although Fowles does not cite it, exemplifies countersupporting, whether it is read as an individual encounter or as a symbol of social tendencies: *The Collector* demonstrates the Many and the Few are constructed entirely with reference to one another, and exist in each other's orbit.

The early phase of Fowles's literary development was exploratory. He was concerned as much with philosophy as with storytelling, and conceived his fictions as vehicles for his ideas. He published *The Aristos* partly to put his thoughts before the world, but also to demonstrate his wish to experiment with a diversity of genres, to refuse 'to walk into the cage labelled "novelist" ' (*A.* 7). Fowles was aware that the style of the book might alienate readers; its short paragraphs each directly expressed an abstract thought, with no connecting narrative flow. However, the first edition of *The Aristos* carried the revealing subtitle *A Self-Portrait in Ideas*, which, many years later, Fowles recognized was still the best description of the book (*A.* 11). As he wrote to his agent on 13 February 1964, he was offering his ideas to his audience not to be judged as a professional philosopher but as a fellow human being expressing himself: 'The "self-portrait in ideas" is both the main purpose of the book and, it seems to me, the best selling line. I've already told Tom [Maschler, his editor] that I don't want it "assessed" by lynx-eyed A. J. Ayerses but by ordinary medium intelligences' (UM). Fowles's objective was self-expression – but not through style, plot, and the other devices of the novel form. Instead, in direct contrast to *The Collector* and *The Magus*, he sought to frame his beliefs as plainly as

27

possible: 'to suppress all rhetoric, all persuasion through style. [. . .] I do not want my ideas to be liked merely because they are likeably presented; I want them to be liked in themselves' (*A*. 13).

A section of *The Aristos* was provocatively entitled 'The Style is not the Man' (*A*. 191–2); Fowles reiterated this belief in his 1970 essay 'My Recollections of Kafka', where he argued against the fashion for finding a literary voice: 'Since so much of literary criticism is devoted to influence tracing and textual analysis, there has arisen an unreasonable demand for instant recognizability' in the artist's work (*W*. 141). To strive to be recognizable in the instant of first reading is to wish to be seen only with the most superficial of glances – with the eye of a consumer seeking to buy, or of a reviewer seeking to enforce commercial trends. Fowles, as the stylistic differences between *The Magus*, *The Collector*, and *The Aristos* demonstrate, was in the early period of his career seeking to be read not for a distinctive voice but through the *phos* or whole sight that his texts tried to suggest was an authentic means of viewing the world. In the next phase of his development (which I am calling his middle period, roughly 1966–79), he would extend his experiments with multiple styles and voices to encompass the range of personas adopted by the author himself in the text. As his best-received novel *The French Lieutenant's Woman* was to show, the author's 'voice' became not an irritating literary fashion to be overcome, but a source of creative fertility – another counter to be manipulated in the godgame.

3

Middle Period: 1966–1979

It started four or five months ago, as a visual image. A woman stands at the end of a deserted quay and stares out to sea. That was all. [. . .] It was an interference, but of such power that it soon came to make the previously planned work seem the intrusive element in my life. This accidentality of inspiration has to be allowed for in writing, both in the work one is on (unplanned development of character, unintended incidents, and so on) and in one's work as a whole. Follow the accident, fear the fixed plan – that is the rule. (*W.* 14–15)

Fowles's work during the late 1960s and 1970s betrays his allegiance to chaos, flux, the play of probability; in his own terms, *keraunos*, the hazard that drives the godgame of writing. In the autumn of 1966, he was midway through composing a novel when, apparently by chance, the vision of the woman on the quay entered his imagination and refused to disappear. Gradually, as Fowles dwelt upon her, she became Victorian and ostracized, 'An outcast' (*W.* 15). Eventually, he abandoned the novel he was working on, and created a new one out of the image. He transformed the visionary woman into Sarah Woodruff, the penniless, fallen governess who is the heroine of *The French Lieutenant's Woman.*

The new novel was to become Fowles's greatest critical success, despite his expectation at the time of writing that it would be received badly: 'Sentences from vitriolic reviews floated through my mind' (*W.* 25). Fowles's anxiety arose because of the daring nature of his project – the novel was an affectionate parody of nineteenth-century fiction such as that of Hardy and the sensation novelists, which copied some of their style but adopted a twentieth-century narrative viewpoint.

29

Despite Fowles's fear that such a mixture would confuse readers and alienate reviewers, the text's blend of the modern and Victorian was extremely successful. In the opening chapter, the narrator describes the Cobb (or harbour breakwater) at Lyme Regis in the following way:

> Primitive yet complex, elephantine but delicate; as full of subtle curves and volumes as a Henry Moore or a Michelangelo; and pure, clean, salt, a paragon of mass. I exaggerate? Perhaps, but I can be put to the test, for the Cobb has changed very little since the year of which I write; though the town of Lyme has, and the test is not fair if you look back towards land.   (*FLW* 10)

Here, while seeming to describe the scenery, the narrator invites the reader to understand what he is doing. His cultural references extend both beyond and before the Victorian age (Henry Moore and Michelangelo); he may seem to write in an over-elaborate style some of the time, but to do so is to imitate the many-tiered edifice of much nineteenth-century descriptive prose ('pure, clean, salt, a paragon of mass'). Moreover, his questioning of his own style ('I exaggerate? Perhaps') is followed by an invitation to set the novel against the reader's preformed impressions of both Victorian and contemporary reality ('but I can be put to the test'). By setting out his method and showing what he requires of his reader, the narrator paves the way for the rest of the novel. The story foregrounds a large number of difficult issues of the period – the controversy surrounding Darwin's theories of evolution, the question of the status of women, the rights of the emerging lower-middle class (personified by the servant Sam, who has ambitions to become a small businessman) – but puts them in the context of a love story that is both Victorian and contemporary: Victorian, because of society's expectations of morality, duty, and chastity, which turn the protagonists into social pariahs when they fall in love, and contemporary because of the way in which their relationship is psychologized, sexualized, and framed in terms of the existentialist project of self-realization. The reader is invited to work out the relationship between the Victorian age and our own, and to question the stereotypes that inhabit both: '*we* have sex thrown at us night and day (as the Victorians had religion)' (*FLW* 259; emphasis in original). As a result, the dividing line between the Victorian century and our own time begins to break down – the novel implies that certainly the Victorian age was different from ours, but that much of the *perceived* difference is illusory, as it emerges from our own period's ideological blindness. *The French Lieutenant's Woman* is a novel of transgressions. These are not only social and sexual, demonstrated in the love affair between the protagonists, but also literary; in style and plot, it is neither a Victorian nor a twentieth-century text, but hovers between them, forcing the reader to evaluate which elements, if any, definitively belong to either age.

Like many novels of either century, *The French Lieutenant's Woman* is a tale of love against the odds. Sarah's main crime against Victorian morality is to have lost her reputation through the rumour that she has slept with Varguennes, the French sailor of the title. She begins the novel standing on the quay at Lyme Regis, ostensibly pining for the departed Varguennes, her appearance exactly as in Fowles's mental image. Charles Smithson, a visiting nobleman who is engaged to the daughter of a rich tradesman, sees her there. Throughout the novel, he pursues the seductive, enigmatic Sarah, but is continually frustrated in his search, as she either evades his understanding or disappears. Only once do Charles and Sarah make love. It is then that he discovers she is a virgin, and the story of the affair with Varguennes is a lie she has concocted. Sarah's fictions are part of her mystery; she is as mendacious as Lily in *The Magus*, and both heroines share the fascinating, unattainable allure of a *princesse lointaine*.

Part of Sarah's fascination, and part of the novel's commitment to *keraunos*, is that we never know, even at the end, what will happen to her. Like *The Magus*, *The French Lieutenant's Woman* refuses to determine the destinies of the protagonists. The narrator announces that, in order to preserve Charles's and Sarah's personal freedom, he will show two possible endings to the story; both appear in the text. In the first, the two protagonists are united, and have a daughter; in the second, which follows immediately, they are separated, after their final dialogue takes a different turn. With a typically Fowlesian allegiance to hazard, the narrator decides the order of the two endings by tossing a coin (*FLW* 390). He is, he believes, a new type of novelist – not a Victorian omnipotent controller of the fiction, but an existentialist one, whose first principle is freedom (*FLW* 99).

Although the narrator poses as the author when explaining these things to the reader, it would be unwise to believe that his words represent a simple biographical account by Fowles of his own creative process. In fact, far from tossing a coin, Fowles originally wrote only *one* ending, the 'happy' variant. In the second draft, he introduced the 'unhappy' variant, but placed it first. He was persuaded to reverse the order for the third draft (thus reaching the sequence of endings in the published version) by Tom Maschler, his editor in London (*Con.* 127), plus his 'sternest editor', his wife Elizabeth.[1] She was a highly influential critic of all his early drafts: 'wives know far better than anyone else the extent to which texts are lived in the writer's mind' (*W.* 168). Although Fowles took very seriously 'the real presence of the woman the novelist shares his life with' (*W.* 166), he also had a considerable interest in the fantasy-women of his novels. He claims that the male novelist's wife may well accuse him of 'imaginative infidelity' (*W.* 168), as Elizabeth no doubt did. So, although her advice may explain the *order* of the endings, Fowles's reasons for composing a dual ending in the first place may have had more to do with the promptings of other female figures in the recesses of his psyche. Eight years after publication, he offered an explanation somewhat different from that in the novel: 'from early in the first draft I was torn intolerably between wishing to reward the male protagonist (my surrogate) with the woman he loved and wishing to deprive him of her – that is, I wanted to pander to both the adult and the child in myself' (*W.* 169). Fowles's argument is based on his theory of the male novelist's M(other)-fixation, which I discussed in the previous chapter with reference to *The Collector*. Sarah is the ultimate incarnation in Fowles's fiction of the unattainable woman; her combination of desirability and inaccessibility clearly energizes the narrative. Evidence for a connection between Sarah and Fowles's sexual fantasies is abundant; he confesses, 'I began to fall in love with her' (*W.* 15). Sarah's many sexually charged, though unconsummated, outdoor meetings with Charles take place in the wooded clearings of the Undercliff at Lyme Regis, near which Fowles lived when composing the novel.

Fowles's Freudian account of fantasy, desire, and deliberate non-consummation, based on the conflict between the novelist as 'adult' and 'child', sounds like a plausible explanation for the structure of his novel, but it is very difficult to state categorically that it is more valid than the narrator-cum-novelist's account of tossing the coin, which, after all, shows a highly Fowlesian commitment to hazard and existential freedom. Here we come up against a major difficulty for any reader trying to relate Fowles to his work: Fowles's self-portraits in *The French Lieutenant's Woman* and elsewhere vary widely, and sometimes contradict one another. Some are ironic, some serious; some reflect his interest in self-reflexive literary games of chance, some lean towards the deterministic doctrines of psychoanalysis. Despite this, they share one consistent element; they show a writer who knows that he is not entirely in control of himself or his fiction. This fits in well with Fowles's declared acceptance of hazard. His rejection of the 'fixed plan' and his acceptance of 'unplanned development of character' can apply not only to the growth of the text during composition, but also to the development of the author himself. Bertolt Brecht, the German playwright, claimed that 'nobody can be identically the same at two unidentical moments. Changes in his exterior continually lead to an inner reshuffling. The continuity of the ego is a myth. A man is an atom that perpetually breaks up and forms anew.'[2] In a more recent, poststructuralist account of identity, the French theorist Jacques Derrida has argued: 'Metaphor shapes and undermines the proper name. The literal meaning does not exist, its "appearance" is a necessary function – and must be analysed as such – in the system of differences and metaphors.'[3] What Derrida and Brecht mean, taken together, is that a person's name is a mere metaphor for a complex, ever-shifting entity that has no continuity over time. *The French Lieutenant's Woman* investigates the same ideas. It shows how the storytelling ego is an ever-fracturing Brechtian atom (with a repertoire of highly Brechtian alienation techniques, such as footnotes and continual intrusion into the story to offer his own anachronistic opinions of his Victorian characters). The narrator's various appearances in the novel contradict one another; having claimed that he cannot see into Sarah's mind, he goes on to produce a lengthy analysis of her mental state as based on 'sexual repression' and 'a pitiable striving for love and security' (*FLW* 226, 229). At other points, he divides like a sort of literary amoeba, becoming at once both a flashily dressed impresario who enters the action and another disembodied voice that continues to narrate outside it. The narrator seems to improvise, doing whatever suits him, or the story, at any moment. He writes, 'Who is Sarah? Out of what shadows does she come?' (*FLW* 96), and follows his own melodramatic enquiry with the self-mocking 'I do not know' (*FLW* 97).

Likewise, the 'Fowles' inferred by the reader is a hazy, shifting, self-contradictory presence, a proper name in the sense understood by Derrida – part of a 'system of differences and metaphors' rather than a simple label for a stable author with fixed opinions and transparently readable ideas. Fowles, committed in his youth to existentialism and in his later years to critical self-reflection, certainly believes he has a real, authentic self, but recognizes that as soon as it is translated into fiction it becomes something else, a persona surrounded by invisible inverted commas. From *The French Lieutenant's Woman* onwards, Fowles's solution to the problem has been to make the number and instability of the many incarnations of the public 'John Fowles' work to his advantage, by creating fictional author-figures who are so much in the foreground that the reader must debate the question of the author and his identity, precisely because his textual personas are not authentic. Fowles expects this kind of questioning from the reader. In 1973, he wrote: 'Only very naïve readers can suppose that a novelist's invented personages and their opinions are reliable guides to his real self.' Instead, the novelist's 'private self has to be subjugated to the public master of a novel's ceremonies', the 'Fowles' in inverted commas (*W.* 31).

Fowles's concerns about the role of the author at this time were not surprising, given the intellectual climate in which he was working. In 1968, Roland Barthes first published the notorious and still highly influential essay 'The Death of the Author'. He argued that the author as we know it was a worthless, empty metaphor – in effect, that the author was dead.[4] A contemporary of Barthes, Michel Foucault, claimed in his essay 'What Is an Author?' (1969) that the author was not

34

an individual but a socially produced function, like a brand name, that existed to make sense of groups of books, and to give a canonical authority to those works selected by the powerful and educated as worthy of study.[5] Fowles remains ambivalent towards such ideas. Jan Relf, in her introduction to *Wormholes*, has pointed out that, despite his frequent attacks on professional critics, his tone is often 'tongue-in-cheek' and that his work 'bears witness to his more-than-competent grasp of deconstruction and poststructuralist theory.'[6] In one memorable juxtaposition from *The Tree*, Fowles derides academics as 'faculty hens and cocks' scratching over the 'purely intellectual midden' of 'literary influences and theories of fiction' (*T*. 36), having in the same paragraph already mentioned that he visited Sweden 'to lecture on the novel' (*T*. 35). Fowles, then, is arguably complicit in the international critical academy even as he seeks to keep a sceptical distance from its theories. In his autobiographical lecture given at the John Fowles symposium in 1996, he offered the following compromise: 'I'm not just blockishly against deconstruction – please believe me. I see there is something there; but for me it is both enough (certainly with Barthes and much of Kristeva) and yet not enough' (*W*. 86).

Fowles's refusal to embrace academicism extends to his approach to fiction. *The French Lieutenant's Woman* demonstrates extreme faith in the fiction-maker's intuition. It is an attempt to recreate the Victorian world, not scientifically but imaginatively, without slavishly following a fixed order or plan:

> You may think novelists always have fixed plans to which they work, so that the future predicted by Chapter One is always inexorably the actuality of Chapter Thirteen. But novelists write for countless different reasons [. . .] Only one same reason is shared by all of us: *we wish to create worlds as real as, but other than the world that is*. Or was. This is why we cannot plan. We know a world is an organism, not a machine. (*FLW* 98; emphasis in original)

The French Lieutenant's Woman's narrator-cum-novelist, with his ever-shifting repertoire of personalities, belongs to the text's unplanned, organic world; during composition, Fowles wrote himself a memorandum stating, '*You are not the "I" who breaks*

35

into the illusion, but the "I" who is a part of it' (W. 20; emphasis
in original). By creating such an imaginative, world-creating
authorial persona, and yet exposing him as just another part of
the fiction, Fowles neatly combines the pose of a Romantic
visionary creator, making a whole world flesh through the
power of his imagination, with the experimental, self-reflexive
stance of the French *nouveau roman*.

The French Lieutenant's Woman is not *un nouveau roman* in the
French sense (that is, by Fowles's own definition, a fiction
actively seeking new narrative structures out of the belief that
to write in traditional ways has become impossible). Fowles
believes that 'with a handful of exceptions' the practice of the
nouveau roman is, 'to us backward British, bewilderingly dull'
(W. 51). Instead, his novel creates new forms out of an ironic
dialogue between novelty and tradition. Fowles's narrator
attempts, self-mockingly, to be dull in a stolid, traditional
Anglo-Saxon academic way, eschewing the flashy, experimental tediousness of the *nouveau romancier*. He takes time to
remind the reader, through knowingly ponderous asides and
footnotes, of such 'facts' as the number of brothels in London,
or nineteenth-century sexology's patriarchal, patronising construction of hysteria as faked symptoms brought on by a
woman's craving for attention. Ironically, this academic clum-
siness, when used as a device to break the novel's gripping
narrative, was shockingly new in the mainstream English
novel in 1969. As a result of this mixing of Romanticism,
experiment, and parodic scholarliness, Fowles is impossible to
pin down in the text. The reader is forced towards Roland
Barthes's conclusion that the author is dead, but paradoxically
is pushed in this direction through the very number of the
author's declarations of his own existence. In effect, Fowles has
become the *deus absconditus*, or absent creator, referred to in
The Aristos. Because the text offers no definitive author, the
reader is free to decide what to do with the 'Fowles' he or she
constructs when reading the novel.

The reader is equally free to construct the protagonists. It is
no coincidence that a recent guide to literary theory, in a
chapter on the poststructuralism of Roland Barthes and the
death of the author, argues that two examples of 'free'
characters who can, in a sense, be written by the reader are

Hardy's Tess Durbeyfield, from *Tess of the D'Urbervilles*, and Sarah Woodruff. They are women 'composed of images set up by the male gaze';[7] this gaze is implicitly also that of the reader. (This turns the reader into a man – or, more accurately, forces him or her to identify with the position of observer/voyeur that is traditionally given to males in our culture. This is a problem that has perplexed and frustrated some female and/or feminist critics of Fowles; I will return to the issue of gender in my next chapter.) Hardy's work can, to some extent, be used to support the argument that the author was dead before Barthes declared him to be so. Hardy, by making Tess a heroine who is what the reader sees in her, renounced his authority over his protagonist in the way that Fowles did when creating Sarah many years later: 'I would have you share my own sense that I do not fully control these creatures of my mind' (*FLW* 99).

The French Lieutenant's Woman demonstrates that Fowles is aware of poststructuralist ideas such as those of Barthes, but, at the same time as adopting them, he implies that they have precedents in the most seemingly traditional literary texts such as *Tess*. After boldly declaring that 'I live in the age of Alain Robbe-Grillet and Roland Barthes', the narrator adds an ambiguous comment that can either mean his text is so ground-breaking that it moves beyond the novel form, or that it is, despite its experimental appearance, close to the Victorian tales it parodies: 'if this is a novel, it cannot be a novel in the modern sense of the word' (*FLW* 97). Likewise, in 'Notes on an Unfinished Novel', his essay on the composition of *The French Lieutenant's Woman*, Fowles expresses the view that the twentieth-century existentialist philosophy of freedom embodied in the behaviour of the protagonists, and explored in his two previous novels, was not entirely an anachronism, but was relevant, *avant la lettre*, to the Victorian age, which was 'existentialist in many of its personal dilemmas' (*W*. 18). In going back to the past for his subject matter and aspects of his style, Fowles was demonstrating his profound unease towards his own, supposedly post-literate period of history: 'One has the choice of two views: either that the novel, along with printed-word culture in general, is moribund, or that there is something sadly shallow and blinded in our age' (*W*. 29).

Writing a novel, especially one looking back to the Victorian era, was itself a deliberate anachronism, part of Fowles's search for whole sight in a blinded age; the irony of the text's treatment of both the nineteenth century and its own time helped to avoid nostalgia. Writing himself afresh as a fluid, chameleon-like narrator of many parts was an opportunity for the author of *The Collector*, *The Aristos*, and *The Magus* to reassert his faith in the organic mutability of the artist's creative life. Charles ends the novel without Sarah, but 'he has at last found an atom of faith in himself, a true uniqueness, on which to build' (*FLW* 445). Fowles, at this point in his career, was a late-twentieth-century version of his own protagonist, an atom splitting and reforming itself in new fictional guises in an effort to find new ways of writing without losing its sense of a vital connection with literary tradition.

Fowles's dialogue with tradition continued in *The Ebony Tower*, a collection of short stories, whose working title was *Variations*. Oddly, given that the collection is a series of experiments with already tested narrative devices (it retells medieval romances, recycles its own themes from story to story, and revisits ideas already worked on by Fowles in earlier fictions), this title was rejected by the readers at Jonathan Cape, his publishers. 'The Ebony Tower', which became the title story once an alternative to *Variations* had been found, is a reworking of *The Magus*. Its equivalent of Nicholas Urfe is David Williams, an art critic and painter of minor abstracts, who visits the ageing Henry Breasley, a more significant, more figurative artist. Breasley, a coarser, less articulate version of Conchis, lives in a *ménage à trois* with two young women at Coëtminais, his isolated villa in the Breton forest. David falls in love with one of the women, Diana (known as the Mouse, Breasley's nickname for her, which he derives from Muse), and contemplates leaving his wife for her. However, Diana refuses David's advances, and, on the morning of his departure, leaves without saying goodbye. The other stories also involve loss and the disappearance of something or someone valuable. This disappearance sometimes creates an unsolved mystery, one of Fowles's favourite themes, a continuation of his early fascination with the *deus absconditus*. 'Eliduc' is Fowles's translation of one of the twelfth-century *lais* of Marie de France, in which Eliduc, a young French knight, travels to England and begins an adulterous love affair. On hearing that he is married, his mistress faints and seems to die, but is magically brought back to life by the wife; ultimately, though, he loses both women, as they all take religious orders. In 'The Cloud', Catherine, a troubled woman, vanishes on holiday in France. In 'The Enigma', it is a Conservative MP who disappears. In 'Poor Koko', a literary critic is burgled and has the notes to his new book burnt in front of him. Through its reworking of its themes and influences, *The Ebony Tower* embodies obsessive repetition, the playing-out again and again of the same basic subject matter. Such repetition had become by this stage a theme in itself for Fowles, linked to his interest in the creative process: 'One enigma about all artists, however successful they may be in worldly or critical terms, is the markedly repetitive nature of their endeavour, the inability not to return again and again on the same impossible journey' (*W*. 164). The collection's stories are not to be taken separately; they are variations upon one another, avatars of the medieval romances that fascinated Fowles while at university. In 'A Personal Note', which precedes 'Eliduc', he writes that such stories as those of Marie de France may seem naïvely constructed, but no writer can dismiss them, because 'He is watching his own birth' (*ET* 119). The reworked romances of *The Ebony Tower* form Fowles's own genealogy of his fiction, a sketch of his literary origins.

Fowles's attitude towards these origins is not entirely uncritical. David Williams's struggle with Breasley represents not only the young knight's conflict with the guardian of the princess, so typical of medieval tales, but also Fowles's own struggle to emerge from the influence of those tales themselves. However reverent Fowles may have been towards medieval romance and its archetypes, he had to find some way to move beyond them in order to progress as an artist without divorcing himself from his roots by resorting to the inorganic, gutless art of the *nouveau roman*, signified by the painting of David Williams, with its polite, fashionable 'abstraction' from real life (*ET* 113).

The Ebony Tower was a partial move in this direction, but a more definitive reworking of romance appeared in 1977: the sprawling *Daniel Martin*, both a *Bildungsroman* and an account of the development of one generation of Oxford graduates. This novel shares familiar romantic features of love, loss, and the quest for renewal; as a young man, Daniel, the protagonist, sleeps once with Jane, but marries her sister, Nell. He eventually realizes that he has 'picked the wrong sister' (*DM* 690) and, after relationships with a number of other women, creates a life with Jane. Although these affairs do dominate the novel, it is an attempt by Fowles to broaden his horizons, addressing the development of one section of society rather than a hero alone. The first chapter offers scenes of rural life reminiscent of Hardy, 'without past or future, purged of tenses' (*DM* 16), but this evoked pastoral world is not a mere Arcadia, disconnected from social reality. Instead, it is linked clearly to history in the form of the Second World War – Dan looks up and sees a German bomber in the sky (*DM* 11). Even in this first chapter, Dan's identity is split between an 'I' who writes from a later perspective and a 'he' who is supposed actually to *have* the early experiences. The relationship between the two is very close, but there are suggestions that the later Daniel is manipulating the earlier one almost like a puppet: 'I feel in his pocket and bring out a clasp-knife' (*DM* 16). The later Daniel is also situating the earlier one as the subject of a history – a narrative that positions its protagonist in an evolving social context.

In such a huge novel, this context is evidenced in innumerable ways. Here, I will follow one example; Dan's relationship to the cinema. Dan harbours ambitions to become a novelist (which are fruitless, as he eventually admits to himself); he begins his literary life as a playwright, then turns to screen work. This begins to alienate him from some of his old Oxford friends:

> They couldn't understand why I should want to get involved in such a corrupt *demi-monde*, why play-writing was not enough . . . or so [Nell] said. They certainly didn't say so to my face, though I sensed a growing distance between us, a breakdown of vocabulary and shared values. The cinema also internationalizes; and I began to see them as obscurely provincial. (*DM* 161–62; ellipsis in original)

Dan's shift to a more popular medium is, to his friends Anthony (an Oxford don) and Jane, a betrayal of a certain traditional, moral view of culture derived from Matthew Arnold among others. They fear that Dan is, to use Arnold's term (which I take from *Culture and Anarchy*),[8] serving the philistines – becoming a panderer to those who have leisure time and aspirations to culture but no useful education in the humanities or innate sense of taste. *Daniel Martin* takes something from Fowles's own experience of the world of movie production; his 1981 essay 'The Filming of *The French Lieutenant's Woman'* charts his efforts to find a director and scriptwriter for a film adaptation of the novel from 1969 to 1980, a period largely coinciding with the writing of *Daniel Martin*. Fowles claims that in that novel, 'I did not hide the contempt I feel for many aspects of the commercial cinema' (*W.* 44), the chief of these being its blind fetishization of profit. Dan also rails against the medium's ability to compromise the artist's vision:

> The commercial cinema is like a hallucinogenic drug: it distorts the vision of all who work in it. What is at stake behind the public scenes is always personal power and prestige, which reduce the industry to a poker-table where every player must, if he is to survive, become some kind of professional cheat, or hustler. (*DM* 154)

Fowles, despite the reservations expressed here, is far too aware of cinema's possibilities to share completely Dan's spite or his friends' contempt towards the medium. Fowles has argued that film is an important influence not only on *what* contemporary people think, but on 'the *mode* of imagination', or *how* we think (*W.* 23; emphasis in original): 'all our conscious, and unconscious, imaging powers as we read – or dream – are now geared to "seeing" narration in cinematic terms' (*Con.* 80). He claims to have seen an average of one movie a week since childhood (*W.* 23). He wrote the screenplay to the largely unsuccessful film version of *The Magus*, which in Fowles's own words, was 'disastrously awful' (*Con.* 66). *The Collector* and 'The Ebony Tower' have also been filmed, the latter for television. *The French Lieutenant's Woman*, most notably, has been adapted for cinema with a script by the

41

playwright Harold Pinter. *Daniel Martin* in many ways resembles a huge screenplay freed from the studio machine and the constraints of time and length that for Fowles still make the cinema 'at its best a major art' (*W*. 44). Its narrative is full of structural imitations of, and direct references to, 'panning shots, close shots, tracking, jump cuts and the rest' (*W*. 24); 'She looks down; a little pause; a "beat", in the jargon' (*DM* 22); a chapter ends with 'Cut' (*DM* 142). 'Notes on an Unfinished Novel', written in 1967, bravely declared that prose fiction was 'inalienably in possession of a still-vast domain' (*W*. 24) which the cinema could not reach. Fourteen years later, Fowles was much less certain of the boundary between the two arts: 'A good director is always partly a novelist, and vice versa' (*W*. 45). Later still, in 1988, he told Katherine Tarbox that the two media share 'a curious feedback' in which cinema, whose techniques of editing and cutting were originally taken from literature, came in turn to influence the written medium (*Con*. 151). *Daniel Martin* represents Fowles's attempt to situate the novel amid the newly emerging technology which in one sense threatened it as a medium, but in another, gave it a new lease of life. In this context, *Daniel Martin*'s repeated references to the cinema become much more than allusions by Dan to his own work as a screenwriter. Dan moves on from the existentialist autobiographical template established by Nicholas Urfe; he becomes not only the chronicler of the key scenes of his own development, but the narrator of a historical trend, the rebirth of the novel in the celluloid world.

Towards the end of the decade, Fowles intensified his interest in non-fiction. In 1978 he published *Islands*, an essay mainly about creativity, accompanied by photographs of the Scilly Isles by Fay Godwin. This had been preceded in 1974 by *Shipwreck*, a shorter text with photographs by the Gibsons of Scilly. *Shipwreck* and an abbreviated version of *Islands* are anthologized in *Wormholes*. In 1979 came *The Tree*, a polemical ecological essay. Compared to his novels, these works may seem unimportant to the ordinary reader, but they provide great insight into the link between Fowles's life and his work. *Islands* restates some of the themes of erotic loss and separation explored in 'Hardy and the Hag' and elsewhere, but focuses particularly on the trope of the labyrinth (which, as I have mentioned in my account of *The Magus*, is one of Fowles's favourite metaphors for the world and the text). *The Tree* deals with another, similar trope, the forest of endless interconnected pathways and clearings, in which any visitor becomes lost, and is 'the best analogue of prose fiction' (*T*. 79). The wood is a creative space of uncertainty, in which the reader, writer, or protagonist can lose him or herself and find new, unexpected ideas. Fowles's interest in this image stems partly from his long-standing enthusiasm for medieval romance; another key influence here is his passion for the natural world. From being a young man who collected natural specimens 'with both gun and rod' (*W*. 405), the older Fowles turned away from hunting and towards 'less botany than gardening' (*W*. 406). During the Second World War, his family had been evacuated from the suburban claustrophobia of Leigh-on-Sea to Ipplepen, a Devon village he found idyllic. He fictionalized this experience in the first chapter of *Daniel Martin*. His early experience of this bucolic rural environment came to influence his own knowingly disordered style of gardening, in direct opposition to his father's more orthodox sense of cultivation for yield: '[My father] thought it madness to take on such a "jungle", and did not believe me when I said I saw no need to take it on, only to leave it largely alone' (*T*. 26).

These two styles of horticulture are metaphors for different approaches to literary composition: the market-oriented, demand-led method of the professional and the organic, spontaneous creativity preferred by Fowles. The latter approach demands a more egocentric artist, who is more inclined to pursue his or her own whims than to follow the demands of the market. Fowles's commitment to the integrity of the individual and his or her unique way of seeing the world owes something, inevitably, to Romanticism and its fetishization of the sublime and visionary genius (as expressed by Wordsworth, Coleridge and others). As a twentieth-century artist, though, Fowles is continuing another individualistic tradition, that of the high modernism of writers such as James Joyce. Joyce's egocentric method of composition is praised by Fowles in *Islands*, where he writes of Joyce, Homer, and implicitly himself:

43

The real Ulysses is whoever wrote the *Odyssey*, is Joyce, is every artist who sets off into the unknown of his own unconscious and knows that he must run the gauntlet of the island reefs, the monsters, the sirens, the Calypsos and the Circes, with only a very dim faith that an Athene is somewhere there to help and a wise Penelope waiting at the end. (*I*. 74)

Fowles claims that the creative process is an interior voyage of epic proportions. The psychic sailor, implicitly male, encounters a series of female archetypes, from those that distract or ensnare him (Calypso, Circe, the sirens) to those that aid or comfort him (Athene, Penelope).

Some critics tend to sideline such claims, and concentrate on the work itself rather than its relationship to Fowles, in order to place it within a newly emerging postmodernist canon of knowingly *un*original literature. Fowles's historical fictions, *The French Lieutenant's Woman* and *A Maggot*, in particular, have been taken as postmodernist because of their paradoxical combination of self-conscious literariness (where they show the reader that they *are* novels) and their resemblance to non-literary texts such as books by historians or documents from bygone ages. In *A Poetics of Postmodernism*, Linda Hutcheon chooses *The French Lieutenant's Woman* as a prime example of what she calls 'historiographic metafiction', or 'those well-known and popular novels which are both intensely self-reflexive and yet paradoxically also lay claim to historical events and personages'.[9] Historiographic metafiction is supposedly a new form of the novel, distinguished by 'postmodern paradox',[10] or a knowingly self-contradictory balance between self-reflexivity and historical reference. Hutcheon is not alone in adducing paradox or self-contradiction in order to classify Fowles as a postmodernist. Turning to the John Fowles entry in *Postmodern Fiction: A Bio-Bibliographical Guide*, we read: 'John Fowles is a writer attracted to paradox, primarily because he believes that growth comes dialectically from a web of contradictions.'[11] Brian McHale, in a student-oriented reader on postmodernism, cites *The French Lieutenant's Woman* as 'a novel of forking paths' with a 'self-contradictory structure'.[12]

It is certainly true that Fowles's work can be paradoxical, but this may be due more to his individualism and total faith in the unplanned 'organic growth' of the text (*Con.* 88) than to his work's postmodernity. Although he has written two novels set in the past, Fowles rejects 'historical fiction' as a label because he believes that the novel cannot aspire to a scholarly under-standing of bygone times. In 'Past and Present Comment: An Afterword', a piece following a collection of essays by profes-sional historians entitled *Locating the Shakers*, he reserves his praise for academics who study the past, declaring that novelists cannot compete with their scholarship. Instead, 'we may have a special and sometimes acute sensitivity towards [the past], usually in the sense that we can see the present in the past, can jump the passage of real time – we can "feel" some past, some different society and culture' (*LS* 147–8).

Thus Fowles's historical fictions do lay claim to real events, as Hutcheon argues, but only on the basis of the non-rational sensitivity of the individual who wrote them. Hutcheon's postmodern novels, like Brecht's epic plays, seek to teach their audience to be 'thoughtful and analytic, rather than either passive or unthinkingly empathetic'.[13] Fowles, by contrast, wishes his reader to share in his intuitive sensitivity to his material, and not to undertake too much analysis. He has stubbornly refused to explain his work to curious correspon-dents: 'what I wrote is what I meant. If it wasn't clear in the book, it shouldn't be clear now' (*W.* 28). Fowles's statement suggests that the content of his work can be divided into two parts: the 'clear' content and the unclear remainder, which is not meant to be analysed.

This is where Fowles's distance from postmodernism be-comes most apparent. The deliberately obscure elements of his work are rooted in a Romantic celebration of the mysteries of the creative process, a song of the authorial self:

> What matters to writers is not subjects, but the experience of handling them; in romantic terms, a difficult pitch scaled, a storm survived, the untrodden moon beneath one's feet. Such pleasures are unholy; and the world in general does right to regard us with malice and suspicion. (*W.* 28)

Fowles's view of creativity as a solitary mystery to be celebrated arises from his belief that not only the artistic process but also human existence is never fully comprehen-sible to science. Just as he despises the idea that 'a book is like

45

a machine; that if you have the knack, you can take it to bits'
(*W*. 28), so he claims that ordinary experience is 'hopelessly
beyond science's powers to analyse. It is quintessentially
"wild" [. . .] unphilosophical, irrational, uncontrollable, incal-
culable' (*T*. 41). Despite this, Fowles does not see the conflict
between analysis and 'wild' experience as insoluble, because
both can enhance the individual human being's relationship to
the natural world:

> I discovered, too, that there was less conflict than I had imagined
> between nature as external assembly of names and facts and
> nature as internal feeling; that the two modes of seeing or knowing
> could in fact marry and take place almost simultaneously, and
> enrich each other.
>   Achieving a relationship with nature is both a science and an art,
> beyond mere knowledge or mere feeling alone [. . .] (*T*. 43)

Fowles understands the way in which analytic and irrational
impulses can contradict one another in the same person.
Nevertheless, he still believes that a transcendental relationship with nature (transcendental because 'beyond mere knowledge') can resolve the contradiction by making them work
harmoniously together. He does not see their contradictory
coexistence as desirable in itself, as Hutcheon's account of him
as a paradoxical postmodernist would suggest he should.
'Again and again in recent years I have told visiting literary
academics that the key to my fiction, for what it is worth, lies
in my relationship with nature' (*T*. 35). Students and academics
visiting his complex body of work may well feel sceptical
towards any putative 'key' to the *œuvre*, least of all one put
forward by Fowles himself. Nevertheless, Fowles's metaphor
of the wood, sustained in *The Tree*, would certainly support his
view of the importance of nature to his work. If the wood is
the text, it is also the psyche, and wandering in it is a journey
of self-discovery and self-validation, which renders such
simplistic binary classifications as modernism–postmodernism
largely irrelevant.

In *The Tree*, *Islands*, and 'Notes on an Unfinished Novel',
Fowles writes of the *individual* use of language – what
Ferdinand de Saussure, the structuralist scholar of linguistics,
called *parole*, rather than *langue* (by which he meant the entire

linguistic system). Saussure tended to dismiss *parole* as insignificant and ephemeral. Fowles resists this structuralist emphasis on overarching systems of knowledge. He also rejects poststructuralist attempts to claim the author is dead or is a social signifier like a brand name. His individualism dates back to the earliest phase of his writing life, and behind it lies a fear of becoming a standardized, mediocre citizen. Even as early as 1964, in 'I Write Therefore I Am', he expressed this fear; when struggling to become published, he did jobs he disliked because he was afraid that work itself might become too attractive, and he would become 'one of those sad, faded myriads among the intelligentsia who have always had vague literary ambitions but have never quite made it' (*W.* 5–6). Fowles adds that he chose writing in the existentialist sense of choosing; he forever had to make the decision anew and live in fear that it was the wrong one (*W.* 6). His existentialism, his desire to fulfil himself as an individual, came before his decision to write fiction: 'I don't think of myself as "giving up work to be a writer". I'm giving up work to, at last, *be*' (*W.* 7; emphasis in original).

Even as early as 'I Write Therefore I Am', Fowles was beginning to see contemporary trends in writing, and what it meant to be a writer, in cultural and ethnic terms. He attacked those American novels that were well written but had few ideas, and those inferior British fictions that were primarily intended to entertain, being picaresque novels with a contemporary gloss, aimed to create 'what I call the *novel of fun*' (*W.* 9; emphasis in original). In a typically individualist way, he made the existentialist choice to be neither British nor American. This statelessness was expressed not in the simple sense of becoming an exile, but in a refusal to conform to the dominant cultural model imposed on writers by either nation.

Fowles has always been interested in Englishness, but also in foreignness, or, more accurately, what it means to have a sense of oneself as existing somewhere between Englishness and another identity. In 'On Being English but not British' he claims that he identifies strongly with England as a mytho-historical construct, rather than Britain, which is a later political expedient in which he has little interest (*W.* 91). For

Fowles, England and Britain are not geographical places or groups of people: instead, they exist most vividly in the mind. By believing this, Fowles comes close to the position of many postcolonialist theorists, such as Benedict Anderson, who has written about what he calls *imagined* political communities. Anderson argues that such communities 'are to be distinguished, not by their falsity/genuineness, but by the *style* in which they are imagined'.[14] Fowles would not entirely agree with this part of Anderson's theory; for him, Englishness is not a style but a genuine part of his imagination, whereas Britishness is a false, bureaucratically sanctioned ethnic identity – a style in the sense of a mode to which people are forced to conform.

Anglo-Britishness is just one of the dual ethnicities that fascinate Fowles. Frequently, his major characters find themselves displaced out of their native culture. The result is a curious mixture, an in-between stage, in which the individual belongs neither to his or her own nation nor the imitated Other. Charles Smithson, once he loses Sarah Woodruff, is such a person. A passage from *The French Lieutenant's Woman* describes his feelings as a traveller:

> it was boredom, to be precise an evening in Paris when he realized that he neither wanted to be in Paris nor to travel again to Italy, or Spain, or anywhere else in Europe, that finally drove him home.
>
> You must think I mean England; but I don't: that could never become home for Charles again [. . .] It had so happened that on his way from Leghorn to Paris he had travelled in the company of two Americans [. . .] and the American's criticisms, though politely phrased, of England awoke a very responsive chord in Charles. He detected, under the American accent, very similar views to his own; and he even glimpsed, though very dimly and only by virtue of a Darwinian analogy, that one day America might supersede the older species. (*FLW* 411)

Again, such passages connect Fowles to late-twentieth-century theories of ethnicity. The postcolonialist thinker Homi K. Bhabha argues that a person subjected to 'the discriminatory effects of the discourse of cultural colonialism' will not simply discriminate between two cultures, or struggle between two identities. Instead, 'the trace of what is disavowed is not repressed but repeated as something *different* – a mutation, a hybrid.'[15] The hybrid is born of one person's attempt to imitate another culture, but in a way that is doomed to failure precisely because of the underlying cultural difference. Clearly, Charles Smithson, like Fowles's other protagonists, is not a person subjected to colonial discrimination in the sense meant by Bhabha – he does *not*, say, experience racial abuse, or the imposed rules of a 'superior' invading power. On the contrary, he is on the opposite side of the colonial experience; like Fowles himself, he belongs to the dominant, colonizing culture. Nevertheless, there is a sense in which Bhabha's theory of hybridity, somewhat adapted, might usefully be applied to him. Although Charles does in fact return to Britain, at this point in the narrative he is English by birth and accent, but with American views on English hypocrisy and, above all, a sense of identification with America as his natural dwelling place. Earlier on, Charles's Englishness is played ironically against Varguennes's Frenchness, affecting his sense of himself as secure in his identity. By transgressing English morality and becoming Sarah's lover, he is, like her, being made partly foreign, an ethnic Other, a mutant product of two cultural myths, one of chastity and probity (Englishness) the other of sexual licence and transgression (Frenchness). Neither of these may bear any real relationship to people of either nationality, but this does not stop them from affecting Charles deeply. He recoils with shock when he receives a note of assignation from Sarah, written in French: 'The French! Varguennes!' (*FLW* 202). Sarah, too, is a hybrid, at least in her original form; Claire de Duras's 1824 novel *Ourika*, translated by Fowles in 1977 and cited by him as 'the germ of *The French Lieutenant's Woman*' (*W.* 59), is about a talented and beautiful black girl, the Ourika of the title, who grows up happily, adopted by a noblewoman in pre-Revolutionary France, until she realizes that her blackness will forever alienate her from white society: 'I saw myself hounded by contempt, misplaced in society, destined to be the bride of some venal "fellow" who might condescend to get half-breed children on me' (*O.* 14). In 1994, Fowles stated his belief that Sarah was inspired by Ourika, but he unwittingly changed the colour of her skin: 'I'm afraid it has revealed to me a remnant of colour prejudice, since something in my unconscious cheated on the essential clue [to Sarah's origin in

Ourika]. The woman in my mind who would not turn had black clothes but a white face' (*O.*, p. xxx). In the title story of *The Ebony Tower*, David Williams is also ethnically and culturally displaced. In the Breton landscape of Breasley's villa, whose ethnic connotations grow out of the *matière de Bretagne* of medieval romance, his English self-restraint is put to the test by another, more recent French myth, the existentialist credo of self-realization. Like the young Breasley, he finds his ethnic identity is threatened, and seeks 'to hide from whatever in French culture threatened to encroach' (*ET* 82). Unlike Breasley, David is unable to isolate himself in his Englishness, and becomes instead culturally divided between his 'real and daily world' (*ET* 81) – consisting of London suburb, job, and family ties – and the romantic Brittany represented by Coët-minais. David's English identity mutates and hybridizes, creating the displaced, frustrated man we see at the end of the story, who loses both Diana and the illusion of a happy, fulfilled marriage in England. In *Daniel Martin*, Dan's move to Hollywood pushes him out of his Englishness. Dan's girlfriend Jenny narrates his games of pool with his host Abe, in which they jokingly assume American actors' roles taken from the movie *The Hustler*: '[the men were] endlessly arguing about how much "English" to use in their shots. I was cast by Abe as a feed, a Scottish fellow-sufferer. You never knew the only decent thing that came out of that damn country was a crooked way of hitting a pool-ball?' (*DM* 261). Jenny is Scottish and therefore not English; Abe, the American, sees the couple not as unified in Britishness, but as ethnically divided. To have Englishness, or to use 'English' in the game of pool, means to hit the ball askew, to cheat without breaking the rules, to play the game but not in a straight, orthodox fashion; in short, to be both conformist and corrupt. Dan, in Jenny's view, is both of these. He is succumbing to the financial lure of Hollywood, demonstrating how venal an Englishman can be; at the same time, he is repeatedly imitating a Hollywood film character, conforming to a powerful American media stereo-type. He is thus demonstrating the beginnings of a hybrid identity.

Dan's definition of Englishness hints that Fowles was refining the existentialist theories that had sustained his earlier fictions, and in particular, reconsidering them in national/ cultural terms:

> Perhaps all this is getting near the heart of Englishness: being happier at being unhappy than doing something constructive about it. We boast of our genius for compromise, which is really a refusal to choose; and that in turn contains a large part of cowardice, apathy, selfish laziness – but it is also, I grow increasingly certain of this as I grow older, a function of our peculiar imagination, of our racial and individual gift for metaphor; for allowing hypotheses about ourselves, and our pasts and futures, almost as much reality as the true events and destinies. (*DM* 83)

Dan goes on to compare the English to the Americans, who at least look problems squarely in the face and attempt to do something about them. Another comparison might be with the French, the originators of the existentialism studied by Fowles. Frenchness and Americanness, in different ways, both signify a literal-minded, pragmatic, existentially driven mode of being, without the sublimating metaphoric facility of Englishness, that will forever play with a problem linguistically and weave tales around it, rather than confront it. The displaced Englishman in Fowles's novels, then, is a character poised on the threshold between two mental spaces: the typically English self-ignorance that uses metaphors to hide any mental content by calling it something else; and the potentially terrifying realm of self-knowledge, gained with the appropriation of a foreign identity, that offers existential freedom and the possibility of personal growth.

These words, taken from *The Tree*, sum up Fowles's perception of himself at the end of what I have called his middle period:

> So I sit in the namelessness, the green phosphorus of the tree, surrounded by impenetrable misappellations. I came here really only to be sure; not to describe it, since I cannot, or only by the misappellations; to be sure that what I have written is not all lucubration, study dream, *in vitro*, as epiphytic upon reality as the ferns on the branches above my head. (*T.* 93)

On a literal level, Fowles refers to his journey to Wistman's Wood on Dartmoor, a place with significant personal

51

associations, even though he had been there only twice. He recalls his first visit, as a lieutenant of Marines in 1946: 'It was forlorn, skeletal, almost malevolent' (*T*. 86). His father told him a rumour that a man had once hanged himself there, an image of sufficient power and persistence that it would enter his later novel, *A Maggot*. Metaphorically, Fowles alludes to his own position as a writer in 1979. He comes to the tree of his *œuvre*, set in its labyrinthine forest of intertextual influences, not to describe it, for to do so would be to create only another text, another persona, another fragmentation of Brecht's ever-changing atom. Instead he seeks some form of obscure self-validation; to be sure that what he has done is authentic and not mere academic 'lucubration', divorced from reality. In his later work, *Mantissa*, *A Maggot*, and the late essays collected in *Wormholes*, he would come to play with this search for self-validation as another text in itself, a story to be sceptically retold just as *Tess of the D'Urbervilles* was retold by *The French Lieutenant's Woman*, ironized but revitalized by the more mature author he was becoming.

4

Later Period: 1980–2001

'I meant every word I said just then. You've ruined my work from the start, with your utterly banal, pifflingly novelettish ideas. I hadn't the least desire to be what I am when I began. I was going to follow in Joyce's and Beckett's footsteps. But oh no, in you trot. Every female character has to be changed out of recognition. She must do this, must do that. Every time, pump her up till she swamps the whole shoot. And in the end it's always the same bloody one. I. e., you. Again and again you've made me cut out the best stuff. That text where I had twelve different endings – it was perfect as it was, no one had ever done that before. Then you get at it, and I'm left with just three. The whole point of the thing was missed. Wasted.' He turns to look angrily at her. She is biting her lips. 'I can tell you now where I'm setting the next one. Mount Athos.' (*Man.* 126)

Miles Green, the protagonist of *Mantissa* who speaks these words, represents Fowles's most bizarre amalgam of protagonist and authorial persona. He is a novelist who completely loses his memory, then wakes up inside a padded cell, which turns out to be his own brain. The entire narrative takes place in this solipsistic enclosure from which Miles cannot escape. As he recovers his memory, he argues and consorts with a beautiful woman who magically changes – and sheds – her clothes, adopting various disguises and sexual roles (psychiatrist, punk rocker, nymph, geisha). She eventually reveals herself to be Erato, the muse of lyric poetry, whose aim is to inspire Miles to reach new creative heights. Erato performs a variety of sexual acts with Miles, which he finds alternately disgusting and arousing. Their purpose is nominally to allow him to produce his next book; his eventual ejaculation inside her is supposedly a creative completion as well as an orgasm.

Ironically, at the point of climax, the barriers of the padded cell dissolve, and the outside world is revealed – but Miles is too deep in coital bliss to notice. As this suggests, he does not develop either as an artist or as a person, despite his sexual success. Unlike Fowles's previous protagonists, he offers the reader no sense of inner evolution, but remains a shallow and vacuous personality, rather like an older Nicholas Urfe with all the sexuality and self-regard but without any of the redeeming curiosity or the potential for growth that so interested Conchis. Near the end of the novel, Miles lies in bed with Erato. He languidly tells her that 'The curse of fiction' is that there must be 'All those boring stretches between the sexy bits [. . .] I knew we were made for each other then' (*Man*. 159). His sexual Odyssey ends with the bathetic cry of a cuckoo clock.

Mantissa parodies Fowles's earlier fictions, so many of which narrate the existential development of a man and woman arising from their encounter in a confined space. *The Collector* is its most obvious ancestor, but Mantissa simultaneously mimics Charles's and Sarah's dialogues in the Undercliff, and Nicholas's conversations with Lily and Rose in Conchis's *domaine* around Bourani. It is also mock-autobiography, the song of the authorial self remixed into badinage, fake psychoanalysis, deliberately clumsy pornography, and ironic asides on the act of composition. Like Miles Green, Fowles in mid-career saw himself as a literary innovator. He drafted two endings to *The French Lieutenant's Woman* (three, if the initial fantasy ending where Charles marries Ernestina is counted), and their eventual order was suggested by his wife; Miles Green's novel with a dozen endings is ruthlessly cut down by Erato to leave him with a mere three, in a form of literary emasculation. Despite Erato's castrating power as an editor, *Mantissa* is concerned mainly with Miles and his creative potency. It is a phallocentric satire, focused not only on Miles's penis and its sensations, but also on the phallus as a symbol of the right to explore, dominate, and create – fundamentally, to experience *desire* – which is traditionally accorded to males, and denied to females, in patriarchal Western culture.

Mantissa is not the only book by Fowles that subordinates women to male artists, or that has been seen as sexist. Sarah Woodruff runs away from the threat of institutionalization represented by Dr Grogan (the local physician who proposes to confine her to a lunatic asylum) only to become shut up in another patriarchal institution, the Pre-Raphaelite Brotherhood, as model and muse to Dante Gabriel Rossetti. In *The Magus*, Nicholas Urfe is educated by three women (Lily, Rose, Alison), but all are tools of the real teacher, Conchis. Peter Conradi has pointed out that Fowles is 'an apologist for the female-principle much given to imagining the sexual exploitation and salvation of women'.[1] Fowles has often suggested that he has an essentialist view of gender – that is to say, he sees it as innate, part of a person's very being, rather than a socially determined role. He has claimed that 'I see man as a kind of artifice, and woman as a kind of reality. The one is cold idea, the other is warm fact' (*W*. 26); men are active, logical, egotistical, and destructive of nature, whereas women are the opposite. It is this essentialism that some critics see as a barrier to Fowles's claims to be a feminist. Pamela Cooper argues that, despite their appearance of feminism, Fowles's novels confirm 'the woman in her passive, instrumental role relative to art, language, and narrative'.[2] Bruce Woodcock, by contrast, sees 'a critical self-awareness' at work, exposing the contradictions within male ideology, but in a partly self-defeating way that arises from 'blind spots [. . .] in Fowles's own thinking'.[3]

Nevertheless, Fowles has presented himself as a feminist. Speaking to Dianne L. Vipond in 1995, he aligned himself with feminism, but added that his usefulness to the cause was limited by his own inability, as a male, to comprehend either women's position or his own:

> I hope I am a feminist in most ordinary terms, but I certainly wouldn't call myself one compared with many excellent women writers. Part of me must remain male. Masculinity is like the old pea-soup fog, a weather condition I remember from youth. It takes you a long time to realize not only where you are but where you ought to be. True humanism must be feminist. (*W*. 452)

Fowles is aware of the paradox of male feminism. However feminist he would *like* to be, he sees himself as lost in the confusion that surrounds masculinity. For the male artist, part of this confusion may be a felt ambiguity about his own gender. In the interview with Vipond, he says he is a woman himself, albeit only in a metaphorical sense, and incompletely. Crucially, he views his androgyny as a spur to his creativity: 'I am a novelist because I am partly a woman, a little lost in mid-air between the genders' (*W*. 435). It seems that, in Fowles's universe, there are essential masculine and feminine principles, but they must exist *together* in the creative artist, or the socially progressive individual. One can adapt Fowles's very useful qualification of his concept of the Few and the Many from *The Aristos*, cited earlier in this book, and apply it to his ideas of the masculine and feminine; the dividing line between the two genders ought to run *within* individuals as well as between them.

If this is the case, then not only can individual gender identity be a complex, often blurred, mix of two principles, but so can sexuality and adaptation to gender roles. I want to argue that if we read Fowles's novels in terms of their deliberate confusion of sexual categories then their treatment of gender relations appears less self-contradictory. Fowles's novels are, to adopt a contemporary critical term, queer texts, whose narrative strategies permit the protagonists to experiment with new sexualities and new mixes of the masculine and feminine, and thus create new selves. I use the term 'queer' not to mean homosexual – and certainly not in a derogatory sense – but in the sense that developed in gender criticism in the 1990s, some of which is known as queer theory. This criticism uses the term to refer not only to lesbian and male homosexual narratives, but sometimes also in a wider sense, to texts that refuse to take for granted received ideas of gender and sexuality. If we read Fowles's novels through queer theory, it is possible to argue that the existential progress of the protagonists (male or female) is not blocked by Fowles's phallocentric essentialism, but is instead enabled by an exploration of deviance that questions society's ideas of masculinity, femininity, and sexuality. Whatever Fowles has claimed about the essential male and female principles, much of his fiction, especially *Mantissa*, endorses the claim of queer theorist Judith Butler that 'the gendered body is performative [which] suggests that it has no ontological status apart from the various acts which constitute its reality'.[4] This does not mean that gender is a free-for-all; far from it. For Butler, the actions that create gender are socially enforced by powerful codes. Fowles knows this also – Sarah Woodruff's ostracization as a fallen woman is a typical demonstration of the power of taboo. However, he offers his protagonists, at least, the chance of sexual freedom; they perform acts that enable them to become existentially authentic beings with a newly discovered identity outside the restricting sex/gender roles promoted by society. Sometimes, they even self-consciously exploit these roles; as Katherine Tarbox has claimed of Sarah Woodruff, part of her strategy of self-fulfilment is to manipulate the fallen woman stereotype in order to become 'a trans' (that is, a transgendered individual, a woman living like a man), with 'androgynous appearance and behaviour'.[5] When she makes love to Charles in the hotel room, she summons him there and invites him in, appropriating the traditionally male role of seducer. At the same time, Charles is manœuvred into the position of the fallen woman, initially passive but in the end unable to restrain his desire, despite the bond of his engagement.

The Magus, The French Lieutenant's Woman, and *A Maggot*, like Fowles's other fictions, explore a wide range of transgressive sexualities: sadomasochism, voyeurism, troilism, sex outside marital bonds, consorting with prostitutes and fallen women, plus suggestions of lesbianism and male homosexuality. In each case, the initiate (Nicholas Urfe, Charles Smithson, Rebecca Hocknell) comes closer to authentic selfhood as a result of participating in the sexual games organized by the magus (Conchis, Sarah Woodruff, Mr Bartholomew). The interaction between magus and initiate may not always include sexual acts, but is always eroticized; their conversation, if it is not a prelude to sex, will certainly dwell on it. The result parallels Michel Foucault's account of the *ars erotica*, or art of sexual instruction, through which erotic knowledge was handed down in ancient cultures, where 'truth is drawn from pleasure itself, understood as a practice and accumulated as experience'.[6] In Fowles's fiction, with its frequent Sadeian overtones, 'excitation' or 'pain' can often be substituted for 'pleasure', but Foucault's structure of the eroticized education of a pupil by a master or mistress remains intact. Sarah Woodruff's lengthy (s)existential instruction of Charles is the most obvious example of this, but the same applies, say, to *The*

Magus, in which Alison, Lily, and Rose act as vehicles for Conchis's teachings about Nicholas's proper role in sex, as well as in life, as a man.

Fowles, as a self-declared feminist, is aware of the social significance of sexual relationships. The exploration of sexuality in his texts is not just about the protagonist (or reader) and his or her gratification, but is part of a sustained examination of the role of the individual in society. According to Foucault, the term 'sexuality' originated in the nineteenth century, and was connected to

> the establishment of a set of rules and norms – in part traditional, in part new – which found support in religious, judicial, pedagogical, and medical institutions; and changes in the way individuals were led to assign meaning and value to their conduct, their duties, their pleasures, their feelings and sensations, their dreams.[7]

Foucault argues that, in Western culture, the self-knowledge of the individual subject has become grounded on its sexuality. Although constituted *as* deviance by the very power that would seek to oppress it, deviant sexuality has the potential to define the self as existentially authentic by virtue of its nonconformity. In Fowles's work, sexual exploration occurs alongside personal growth and the two become co-dependent. The chief exception to this rule is *Mantissa,* which adopts a philosophy of pleasure and inauthenticity close to Oscar Wilde's. Erato's and Miles's quips sometimes resemble cut-price reissues of his dramatic epigrams: 'God, no wonder *The Times Literary Supplement* calls you an affront to serious English fiction' / 'I happen to regard that as one of the finest feathers in my cap' (*Man.* 149). Ironically, the very text that has come in for most criticism for its treatment of gender and sexuality is that in which Fowles sets out to question the connection between sexual experimentation and authentic existence that he had established in his earlier work.

Fowles, in my view, is not a chauvinist but is, in one sense at least, a queer writer. As well as his claim that he is a novelist partly *because* he is in some sense a woman (cited above), he has given his own gender a mobile, adaptive quality: 'I consider myself a sort of chameleon gender-wise' (*W.* 435). One of his poems, 'The Noble Youth of Athens', refers to the use of *male* prostitutes ('boys') in Athens, as opposed to the female ones sought there by Nicholas Urfe (*P.* 14). Fowles, like Nicholas, went there as a young man, but there is no suggestion that the poem is autobiographical; instead, it is a typical example of Fowles's imaginative exploration of unconventional sexual experience, along the lines of the experiments with sadomasochism in *The Magus*, or with pornography in *Mantissa*. Incidentally, Fowles has admitted that he once wrote a pornographic novel, which he burnt as 'an error of bad taste' (*Con.* 191). Fowles's antecedents, as has often been argued, belong to medieval romance and other sources that conform to the sexual conventions of their time; most readings, though, have not recognized the extent to which his texts also depend on the blurring of sexual categories, and the confusing mixture *within* the individual of identities like Man and Woman. Tellingly, Miles Green begins *Mantissa* in a state of genderless amnesia, then awkwardly acknowledges his masculinity:

> With another painfully swift and reducing intuition it realized it was not just an I, but a male I. That must be where the inrushing sense of belowness, impotence, foolishness came from. It, I, it must be he, watched [his wife's] mouth glide down like a parachutist and land on his forehead. (*Man.* 10)

Mantissa is phallocentric, but is well aware of this. It pulls off a remarkably adroit literary trick, by placing masculine desires at the centre of its narrative, and adopting the patriarchal discourse of pornography, only to examine them critically, and – in a number of knowingly crude double entendres – deflate them.

A Maggot recapitulates many of the themes of Fowles's earlier works, especially *The French Lieutenant's Woman*. It is a historical tale set in 1736. A prostitute, Rebecca Hocknell (alias Fanny), is taken on a journey from London to the south-west of England by a mysterious man (alias Mr Bartholomew, later known as His Lordship). Their journey ends in a remote cave. After some very strange events inside the cave, Rebecca ends up pregnant and His Lordship disappears. Rebecca then gives birth to Ann Lee, the woman who, in real history, founded the Shakers, a religious movement given to feminism, pacifism, and celibacy. Ayscough, a sceptical, cynical lawyer who has been sent by His Lordship's father, a Duke, to find him, interrogates the characters who accompanied him on the journey. Almost nothing else can be said about the plot with any certainty, because the witnesses' testimonies contradict one another on many points, forming a confusing web of conflicting accounts of the same events. While in the cave, Rebecca *may* have been raped by the Devil, or taken into what *may* be a starship to meet beings who *may* be time travellers or extraterrestrials, depending on which version the reader chooses to believe (if any). Ayscough, like the reader, often finds himself exasperated by the farrago of bizarre stories presented to him by the various witnesses. The novel's plot is almost comically baffling, and seems intended to be read with a fair degree of scepticism. Indeed, through its title, *A Maggot* announces itself as a personal whim or quirk; the word of course means worm, but is also an eighteenth-century term for a piece of whimsy, an idiosyncrasy.

A Maggot takes a typically idiosyncratic attitude towards its own historical and literary sources. The 'Historical Chronicle' sections of *The Gentleman's Magazine*, a genuine periodical from 1736, reproduced in the novel in their original typeface and pagination (at monthly intervals in the plot, like a marker of time), show that the events of *A Maggot* are supposed to take place simultaneously with a real historical event, the Porteous affair in Edinburgh. Porteous was an army captain who fired on a rioting crowd, killing several people. He was sentenced to death but reprieved. A crowd broke into the Tolbooth (the prison known locally as the Heart of Midlothian) and lynched him. Fowles's choice to make his novel run simultaneously with the Porteous affair, and to announce this through the *Gentleman's Magazine* excerpts, suggests that he is aware of his own work's connection to a canonical historical novel: Sir Walter Scott used the Porteous incident as the starting point for *The Heart of Midlothian* (first published in 1818).

A Maggot, though, never mentions Scott or *The Heart of Midlothian*. Apart from a brief reference by Ayscough to the Porteous verdict (*Mag.* 109), there appears to be no link between the novels except that of temporal coincidence. Fowles has cited Scott's fiction before in his work; in *Daniel*

Martin, Daniel writes a screenplay based on *Ivanhoe*, and recognizes the value of the Marxist critic Georg Lukács's 'masterly new angle on Scott's faults and virtues, on the cunning mediocrity of his gentleman heroes' (*DM* 559). Despite Fowles's awareness of the tradition of the historical novel in English literature and of Lukács's commentary on it, the Epilogue denies *A Maggot* is a historical novel at all: 'this is a maggot, not an attempt, either in fact or in language, to reproduce known history' (*Mag.* 455). The simultaneity of Scott's and Fowles's plots is seemingly a chance event. *A Maggot* may be pointing to this when Ayscough makes his one reference to the Porteous trial – he mentions that the news was brought to him by a certain 'Mr Robert Luck', a schoolmaster and amateur poet (*Mag.* 108). Luck tells Ayscough, much to the latter's irritation, that he was tutor to William Gay, whose pastoral *Eclogues*, he claims, are a faithful portrait of that part of Devon.

These allusions are seemingly just jokes. The coincidental temporal parallel between Fowles's and Scott's novels, and the chance connection with Gay – both presented through the resonantly named Luck – reveal frustratingly little to the reader. A deeper link, though, can be established: Scott's fiction, via Lukács, helps to organize *A Maggot*, acting as a powerful paradigm of historical fiction, a template of what a historical novel *should* do and be. In the words of Lukács himself: 'What is lacking in the so-called historical novel before Sir Walter Scott is precisely the specifically historical, that is, derivation of the individuality of characters from the historical peculiarity of the age.'[8] *A Maggot* conforms to Lukács's model of historical fiction when it treats history as a complex of social forces that restricts the freedom of the individual and his or her way of thinking, effectively forming his or her identity. The attitudes of Ayscough and Jones, for instance, reveal that they are 'like most of us, still today, equal victims in the debtors' prison of History, and equally unable to leave it' (*Mag.* 237). It also follows the pattern of Scott's novels in that it mixes authentic historical figures such as Luck and Gay with invented characters like Rebecca and Ayscough. These are good reasons for the reader to treat with suspicion the Epilogue's claim that the text is merely a whim. This claim is specious, because the power of the Scott/Lukács paradigm is acknowledged, through such comments as the narrator's references to Ayscough and Jones being formed *as individuals* by history, and the Epilogue's account of the historical formation of the modern ego itself, 'from the hard soil of an irrational and tradition-bound society' (*Mag.* 457).

The Prologue performs a different but related trick: instead of concealing a powerful, important source, it foregrounds a marginal one. Fowles mentions a pencil and watercolour drawing of a young woman, from 1683, which he acquired by chance. The drawing, rather in the manner of the mental image of the woman on the quay who became Sarah Woodruff, 'came slowly to haunt me', and the woman's 'refusal to die' (*Mag.* 5) made Fowles link her with Ann Lee, whom he had long admired. Again, as with Scott and the Porteous affair, *A Maggot* presents its connection with a source as a matter of luck. The difference is that Fowles (or his persona) openly reveals his debt to the source. He is able to do this because it is anonymous and 'not of any distinction' (*Mag.* 5).

This draws us to a key element of *A Maggot*; its favouring of marginal historical voices over stronger, socially dominant ones. This again is in the mould of Scott – in *The Heart of Midlothian*, for instance, the speeches and actions of the peasant heroine Jeanie Deans are considerably more significant to the novel than those of the Duke of Argyle. Fowles, like Scott, favours what Linda Hutcheon has called the 'ex-centric', or voices pushed away from the centre towards the margins of history.[9] These include, typically, the discourses of women and social outcasts. The Shakers, as a feminist, celibate religious cult way outside the eighteenth-century mainstream, were ex-centrics *par excellence*. In the Prologue, Fowles claims an affinity with such marginalized visionaries as Ann Lee and his own creation, Rebecca. Like *The French Lieutenant's Woman*, his text began with a mental image: this time, of a group of riders on a deserted skyline (*Mag.* 5). In both the Prologue and 'Notes on an Unfinished Novel', Fowles's reference to an image arising from his unconscious is accompanied by a denial of interest in the historical novel: 'I would not have this seen as a historical novel. It is maggot' (*Mag.* 6); 'I don't think of [*The French Lieutenant's Woman*] as a historical novel, a genre in which I have very little interest' (*W.* 14). This is very unlikely to be coincidence. It suggests a certain consistency on Fowles's part – rather than allow his career to progress by conforming to the conventions of an established literary genre, he is, with typical individualism, denying any debt to the genre and sticking to the imagist, intuitive type of creativity that works for him.

Fowles's aim, despite his stated rejection of the historical novel, was to bring the past to life for the reader in a way apparently untainted by postmodernist irony or scepticism. This was, it seems, his reason for presenting *A Maggot* in the form of extended dialogues: 'Dialogue, however remote in time, always seems more present than ordinary narrative techniques or description. That is why the drama always seems so intensely present, even in its historically most antique form, with the ancient Greeks' (*LS* 149). Fowles's statement places *A Maggot* within a Lukácsian model of historical fiction. Lukács notes the 'new and important role of dialogue' in the nineteenth-century historical novel, and attributes this to Scott.[10] He claims that dialogue allows the contemporary reader to engage more easily with the historical reality of the past (which for Lukács, a Marxist, means the reality of class struggle). *A Maggot* itself, though, appears to contradict Fowles's own point about the presentness of dialogue, by cutting it up with facsimiles of *The Gentleman's Magazine*, for instance, and by making the dialogue reveal nothing definitive about what has happened. The lack of resolution in the novel, where the many voices of the characters are not subsumed beneath the authoritative voice of a historian, could be said to reveal something about the actual *experience* of historical events (because those in the middle of history do not understand it, and their attempts to explain what is happening often contradict one another). However, it also owes something to the model of dialogue developed by the Russian critic Mikhail Bakhtin, in which the interaction of separate styles, idioms, and discourses was the defining characteristic of the novel itself:

The stylistic uniqueness of the novel as a genre consists precisely in the combination of these subordinated, yet still relatively autonomous unities (even at times comprised of different languages) into the higher unity of the work as a whole: the style of a novel is to be found in the combination of its styles; the language of a novel is the system of its 'languages'.[11]

Bakhtin's system of discourses within a novel creates a 'dialogue' between them, which for him is the essence of the novel form. *A Maggot* is both a Bakhtinian novel of multiple, dialogized discourses and a historical fiction at the same time. Fowles's text makes the point that history itself is realized through the dialogues between different ways of speaking and thinking, inhabited by different individuals with different points of view. As Rebecca says to the exasperated Ayscough, 'Thee hast thy alphabet, and I mine, that is all. And I must speak mine' (*Mag.* 317). Although Ayscough later insists, 'Mistress, there is one and only alphabet, that is plain English' (*Mag.* 420), the novel's very structure makes it clear that Rebecca is right – the English language and nation (and the nation's history) are formed out of conflict, meaning not only military wars, but the dialectic between the ideologies and discourses of different classes and subcultures.

Through its Bakhtinian, polyphonic structure of Ayscough's interviews with the witnesses (interspersed with his letters, occasional comments from the narrator and the excerpts from *The Gentleman's Magazine*), *A Maggot* is able to treat Scott's and Lukács's projects sceptically; while making referential claims to relive the struggles of the past, the novel shows the reader how the 'past' it creates for the reader is a highly artificial, dialogic construct. In its foregrounding of its own artifice, *A Maggot* demonstrates the debt it owes to another, quite different paradigm of narrating the past – the self-conscious falsehoods of Daniel Defoe, who wrote such texts as *A Journal of the Plague Year*, which purported to be authentic historical records but were fictions. Even as far back as 1964, citing his influence on *The Collector*, Fowles had recognized Defoe as 'that supreme master of the fake biography' (*W.* 9). The Epilogue to *A Maggot* does acknowledge the debt: 'A Maggot is not at all meant to be in any direct imitation; he is, in any case, inimitable. To following some of what I take to be the underlying approach and purpose in his novels, I happily confess' (*Mag.* 455). Fowles is here confessing to being a liar, albeit a little sheepishly and in a circumlocutory way, designed not to break the news to his reader too bluntly. Mendacity is the essence of Defoe's approach to history – he fakes a past in order to convince the reader. Defoe's penchant for irony and lies extended to his political satires. Within *A Maggot* (*Mag.* 236) the narrator mentions Defoe's famous pamphlet *The Shortest Way with the Dissenters*, which was a literary practical joke. Defoe, who was himself of Dissenting background, wrote in the persona of a reactionary High Tory. He recommended that the country could solve the problem of dissident religions by simply hanging or deporting as many of their practitioners as possible; however, to be reasonable, Defoe argued that perhaps only the ringleaders should be hanged as an example. Many Tories were fooled, 'and declared his pamphlet excellent', including Fowles's Ayscough (*Mag.* 236).

A Maggot borrows from Defoe in playing a similar practical joke; it offers a simple solution to the mystery, only to lead the reader into a trap. Many of Fowles's audience, aware of science fiction, will probably see a starship or time machine in Rebecca's vision, told to Ayscough, of a strange grey cylinder (the maggot) with a panel in its side, banks of flashing lights, and a window that displays a series of changing images. To reinforce the science-fiction allusion, a strange woman in a suit of 'shining silver' (*Mag.* 223), whom Rebecca calls Holy Mother Wisdom, lives inside the maggot; she seems to be a time traveller or an extraterrestrial. However, these conclusions are mere fantasies of the modern mind. Like Defoe's Tories, we are forced by our own mindset to create an interpretation of the text that reveals our own wish to impose our power on others; we patronize Rebecca by trying to uncover the 'fact' behind her fantasy, only to find that we have merely substituted our own fantasy in its place. To read the maggot as a starship is to decode Rebecca's mystical experience in terms of contemporary myths, which have no greater claim on reality, or perhaps even less of one, than Rebecca's religious visions. Even if we refuse the science-fictional solution, and treat Rebecca's religious experience as authentic, we are again closing off the novel, imposing meanings where none may exist. As Katherine Tarbox argues, 'The maggot experience [. . .] is a metaphor of unassigned meaning.'[12] Typically of Fowles's fiction, it is the very *lack* of a solution to the mystery of the maggot that is the narrative's main strength. Rebecca's experience resists any interpretation; the cave is in a structural, narrative sense as well as a literal one, a black hole. William Patrick Day has used the same scientific metaphor to describe the dark, self-sealing world of Gothic fiction, which 'allows no energy to escape, but traps it in a closed system'.[13] Unlike Scott's or Defoe's narratives, *A Maggot* is a similarly self-contained, decentred text, closed to interpretation. The black hole of the cave is a tantalizing substitute for an organizing principle. There is no dominant voice in the text, and it is up to the reader whom to believe. As Fowles put it of Stonehenge – a monument that features in *A Maggot*, as 'Stonage' (*Mag.* 251) – we can 'decipher just enough to be sure it is very important, but never enough to establish exactly what it is saying' (*E.* 9).

The implied author of *A Maggot*, teasing his audience but always refusing it meaning, bears a curious resemblance to Lucifer as depicted in Defoe's *History of the Devil*:

> the Devil is a true posture-master, he assumes any dress, appears in any shape, counterfeits every voice, acts upon every stage [...] the Devil is in [all his parts], more or less, and plays his game so well, that he makes sure work with them all: he knows where the common foible lies, which is universal passion, what handle to take hold of every man by, and how to cultivate his interest, so as not to fail of his end, or mistake the means.
>
> How, then, can it be denied, but that his acting thus *in tenebris*, and keeping out of the sight of the world, is abundantly his interest, and that he could do nothing, comparatively speaking, by any other method?[14]

This is almost a perfect description of Fowles in his later period. Just as he acts out the role of a devilish purveyor of patriarchal wish-fulfilment (the phallocentric fantasist of *Mantissa* and some of *A Maggot*), he also appears to his readers as an angelic deliverer of ethical, serious narratives that have sexuality at their core only as a means to demonstrate the need for the enlightenment of patriarchal society by feminist subcultures like the Shakers.

Fowles's devilment, then, has a serious agenda. *A Maggot*'s plot differs from the Gothic 'closed system' proposed by Day in that it *can* allow 'energy to escape' by creating meaning and bringing about progress. The story's details are indeterminate, but its historical outcome is not. Rebecca may have been raped by Satan, or impregnated by time travellers, or merely have had a roadside tumble with His Lordship's well-endowed manservant (whose name, Dick, aptly complements Rebecca's alias, Fanny – the terms are English slang for the penis and vagina); similarly, His Lordship may have vanished to Hell, to the future, or somewhere else entirely. In a sense, it does not matter; Ann Lee is born anyway and the Shakers are still founded. Like Defoe's Moll Flanders, Rebecca is rescued from whoredom and dejection by a man who causes her to see visions of 'the other Side of time', which she believes are real.[15] Rebecca is uneducated and virtually illiterate, but has taught herself to read the Bible in the brothel where she works. She feels deep shame towards her work as a prostitute, even before His Lordship takes her away; this, combined with her religious background, would seem to predispose her towards a spiritual conversion and a renunciation of her past. This is part of *A Maggot*'s acknowledgement of history in the Lukácsian and Marxist sense; it suggests that, although Rebecca believes that her spiritual rebirth – and pregnancy – are achieved by 'Christ's will' (*Mag.* 427), she may have been *historically* incapable of interpreting her experience in any other way.

In his later fictions, Fowles is retrospectively historicizing the quest for personal and literary authenticity that was the main theme of many of his earlier novels. By 'historicizing' I mean not only treating it as part of the past, a bygone, but also as a source to be reworked – retold, brought up to date, ironized, even parodied if necessary. Like Defoe's Devil, Fowles has mastered a series of postures that serve to mask his absence. His chief means of creating this absence is dialogue, the form shared by *Mantissa* and *A Maggot*. The quest for personal existential fulfilment, instead of the object of Fowles's novels, has become *an* object to be scrutinized and put through the narrative mill to see what emerges. Rebecca and His Lordship both want to escape from their present circumstances, rather than to 'become themselves' in any twentieth-century sense; one vanishes and the other is absorbed into history. Miles

Green and Erato are mere vehicles for a sceptical examination of the act of composition, in which the solipsistic stasis underlying the production of Fowles's earlier narratives of personal progress (or, put another way, the paradox of Fowles's having philosophized extensively about the freedom to be and to do what one wants, in defiance of social convention, while actually having *done* nothing significant except write in isolation) is ironically brought to the fore by setting *Mantissa* inside the soft grey walls of a brain-cum-padded cell.

In *Islands*, Fowles had reflected on the solipsism inherent in composition – for example, in the passage about the lonely voyage of the artist cited in my previous chapter. He took up the theme in his later non-fiction, and infused it with a sense of self-imposed provincial isolation, a justification of his choice to live in Lyme, far from the perceived superficiality of the London *literati* and their salons: 'A large garden owns me – not the reverse – here in Lyme. I behave there as I do with texts, pursuing alternatives' (*W*. 429). Fowles's writing about his chosen region, the south-west, inhabits a tradition, handed down through Thomas Hardy, of faithfulness to a felt landscape and way of life, of the artist as natural historian and chronicler of rural England. Like Hardy's Wessex, Fowles's region is 'fluid-boundaried' and 'as much imaginative as geographical' (*W*. 259). Fowles adopted the role of regional historian in *Shipwreck*, parts of *Islands*, and the later essays 'Thomas Hardy's England' and 'The Nature of Nature'. This had a basis in his daily life; from 1978 to 1988, he was curator of the Lyme Regis (Philpot) Museum, and is still a patron of the Museum. A small publication, *A Brief History of Lyme*, came out of his work there.

Fowles's awareness of the south-west forms a starting point for his meditations on the function of the artist in his environment and ultimately the purpose of man in the world. When he writes about the region, Fowles is not only a historian of the local and particular but also a *thinker* about the area and its specimens, as much concerned with what the south-west can tell us about history, literature and psychology as with the vanished people and voices of the area. Like Thomas Hardy's Casterbridge, which both was and was not the real Dorchester, the centres of Fowles's regional consciousness, Lyme and the Scillies, are points in an imaginative topography as well as features in a real landscape:

> I have always thought of my own novels as islands, or as islanded. I remember being forcibly struck, on my very first visit to the Scillies, by the structural and emotional correspondences between visiting the different islands and any fictional text [. . .] The island remains where the magic (one's arrival at some truth or development one could not have logically predicted or expected) takes place; and it rises strangely, out of nothingness, out of the onward dogwatches, mere journeying transit, in the writing. (*I*. 30)

Fowles uses the Scillies, with their capacity to reveal serendipitous truths, and Lyme (in particular, his garden, with all its forking paths) as symbols of the choices and chances that are so vital to his creative process. In 'The Nature of Nature' (1995), Fowles foregrounds the writer's ability to see a pattern of choices made or not taken:

> All writers make up their own private slang as to what goes on when they write. An important term – at any rate for me, in my own practice – is the *fork* (as in a path), by which I mean a fairly continuous awareness of alternatives, both 'learned' (remembered) and 'fortuitous' (wild), in what is done. [. . .] being allowed to exist within such an infinity of possible variations, the endless bifurcations of the alternative, forms the reality, like some difficult differential equation, that most serious artists have either to worry or rejoice over. (*W*. 425–6)

The particular and the general, the short walk to the orchids of his garden at Lyme and the imaginative journey of the writer, are chronicled and examined by Fowles using the same storehouse of images. In his meditations on creativity, Fowles imagines himself both grower and plant, keeper of the garden and one of its denizens. In the closing paragraph of 'The Nature of Nature', he writes of his prized woodcock orchids, which 'are not meant to flower as far north as this island, but in the warmth of our south-facing coast they do' (*W*. 429). The foreign journey of the young Fowles, recorded in fantastical form in *The Magus*, has come full circle; he implies that he is not meant to be in England, and yet, settled in the warm coast of his particular intellectual and geographical region, he can flourish like the rare refugee plant. His later period is evidence of his garden's continued tenacity and fertility, the 'endless bifurcations' of its organically evolving natural labyrinth.

5

Conclusion: I Exist Still . . .

In 1998, Fowles published *Wormholes: Essays and Occasional Writings*, an anthology of his most significant non-fiction so far, edited by Jan Relf. *Wormholes* takes its title, with knowing irony, both from the scientific usage of 'a hypothetical interconnection between widely separated regions of space-time' and from 'the other sort of wormhole' made by the burrowing insects that accumulate in Fowles's old house and the antique books he collects (*W*. p. viii). The essays within it contain a similar blend of the cosmic and the quotidian; they are fragments of Fowles's idiosyncratic obsessions and quirks, his maggots, but also elements of his knowingly incoherent but nevertheless fascinating philosophy. In 'The Nature of Nature', the final essay in the collection, he writes of *sideros, keraunos, eleutheria* – necessity, hazard, freedom – a trilogy of Greek abstracts off which 'we individuals bounce, carom, and ricochet like pin-table balls' (*W*. 413). Fowles's image of pinball to discuss the human condition is both apposite and self-consciously absurd, fascinating in its incongruity. The blending of seemingly immiscible discourses has always fascinated Fowles, from the mixture of thriller and philosophical reflection in *The Collector* to the combination of science fiction and historical romance in *A Maggot*. He has always been not only a chameleon gender-wise, but a chameleon genre-wise, able to take a literary convention and breed it with another to produce some curious cross-pollinations. Although clear consistent themes emerge in his *œuvre* (the existential quest; the relationship of the sexes; history and time), his art has always been a syncretistic one, able to borrow from different literary and extraliterary traditions what it sees fit in order to evolve. When

71

in 'Notes on an Unfinished Novel' he wrote that to compose an account of two Victorians making love was 'really science fiction' (*W*. 19), he surely had no idea that he would come to write a science-fictional account of the conception of an even earlier baby, the Shaker Ann Lee. And yet, looking back on his novels, *A Maggot* seems hardly surprising; it is an evolved variation upon *The French Lieutenant's Woman*, a different choice taken by a writer just as concerned with the process of composition as he was before, but determined to treat sceptically the human sense of the primacy of individual identity – 'new-born' in Rebecca Hocknell's period (*Mag.* 457) but later to develop into 'our twentieth-century consciousness of and obsession with self' (*Mag.* 460) – that the earlier novel had accepted a little too readily as an evolutionary goal.

In his later period, Fowles has reflected on his own experience, not with the sentimental permissiveness of nostalgia, but with the creative eye of a still fertile and acute literary composer seeking to make new fictions out of old. Throughout this process, he has been influenced not only by his own work but by that of others – nevertheless, he has asserted that 'Chance [*keraunos*] has made me', and not the 'influences' beloved of academics (*W*. 454). Unfortunately, chance, it seems, has made Fowles a novelist no longer. Since the minor stroke he suffered in 1988, and the sudden, premature death of Elizabeth Fowles in 1990, he has published only non-fiction. This change of direction came about partly because of these sad circumstances, but also because of his squeamishness about 'the element of lying' in novels, as he explained in 1995 (*W*. 455). Given Fowles's ability to shift from one literary mode to another, it is hard to see this focus on essays as a radical break. Fowles, as he has always done, is still telling stories about the world and his position within it. This does not mean he is knowingly lying in his non-fiction, but that, just as in the novels, the truth is arrived at by a roundabout, hazardous means, a voyage through a personal labyrinth. This voyage is never an easy one; Fowles is deeply sympathetic to Virginia Woolf's comment that 'Nature and letters seem to have a natural antipathy . . . they tear each other to pieces' (*W*. 419; ellipsis in original). He knows he can never know or render accurately the truth of his own nature or the world, but is compelled by his profession, his *sideros*, to try.

And yet, he implies, the burden of self-discovery and self-explication is not his alone, but falls on all of us. There is an uncanny moment at the end of 'An Unholy Inquisition', the interview that closes *Wormholes*, where Fowles steps out of the dialogic interview mode – walks out of the page, as it were – to address the reader rather than his interlocutor, Dianne L. Vipond: 'Still . . . still. I exist *still* as I write this, you exist *still* as you read it. Can't you sense a mystery, a precious secret told to you alone, in that word?' (*W.* 456; ellipsis and emphasis in original). In these, the final words of *Wormholes*, Fowles is writing to all his readers collectively but seeming to address each one individually. In the polysemic word *still*, the mysterious stasis of Zen-like existence in the Now (I am still, meaning motionless and contemplative) is counterpointed by a sense of continuity with the past (we are still here) and yet also of imperfection, creating desire for a better future (we are still, that is static – we have not progressed). Fowles's shift away from the existentialism of his early work and towards a more reflective approach to existence is exemplified by the ambiguity of this carefully highlighted word, which resists a simple interpretation, instead encouraging contemplation in the reader. If his comment that 'you exist still' is a mystery told to each reader 'alone' is to make any sense, then it means that it is up to each member of his now vast audience to resist any existentialist quick fix, and to stop and think in order to solve the mystery of their situation for themselves.

A Maggot encourages us to be wary of rampant individualism, 'the Devil's great I, in Shaker terminology' (*Mag.* 460). Fowles's later fiction and essays imply that he is only one human being among many, constantly striving to make responsible decisions on the basis of information that emerges from the following contradictory perceptions: those sensations derived from the contemplation of present nature; an awareness of his connection to past history; and a restless sense of his failure to meet the needs of a dynamic future. If his work tells us anything, it is that we as readers must accept the same responsibility, to advance into a new century by creatively reworking our past, whilst never losing sight of the mysterious present all around us, meaning especially the nature in which we are immersed, and of which we are each a tiny but significant part.

73

Notes

CHAPTER 2. EARLY PERIOD: 1951–1965

1. Gilles Deleuze and Félix Guattari, *A Thousand Plateaus: Capitalism and Schizophrenia*, trans. and foreword Brian Massumi (London: Athlone Press, 1988), 21.
2. Umberto Eco, *Reflections on the Name of the Rose*, trans. William Weaver (London: Minerva, 1994), 58.
3. John Fowles, foreword to H. W. Fawkner, *The Timescapes of John Fowles* (London: Associated University Presses, 1984), 9.
4. Fowles's letter to H. W. Fawkner, cited in ibid. 15.
5. Shyamal Bagchee, '*The Collector*: The Paradoxical Imagination of John Fowles', *Journal of Modern Literature*, 8/2 (1980–1), 219–34.
6. Sigmund Freud, 'The Uncanny' (1919), *The Standard Edition of the Complete Psychological Works of Sigmund Freud*, xvii. 1917–19, trans. James Strachey (London: Hogarth Press, 1955), 217–56, at 234.
7. Gilbert J. Rose, '*The French Lieutenant's Woman*: The Unconscious Significance of a Novel to its Author', *American Imago*, 29 (Summer 1972), 165–76.
8. Michel Foucault, *Discipline and Punish: The Birth of the Prison*, trans. Alan Sheridan (London: Peregrine, 1979), 209.
9. Jacques Lacan, *Écrits: A Selection*, trans. Alan Sheridan (London: Routledge, 2001), 7.

CHAPTER 3. MIDDLE PERIOD: 1966–1979

1. Elizabeth Mansfield, 'A Sequence of Endings; the Manuscripts of *The French Lieutenant's Woman*', *Journal of Modern Literature*, 8/2 (1980–1), 275–86, at 278 n.
2. Bertolt Brecht, *Brecht on Theatre*, ed. and trans. John Willett (London: Eyre Methuen, 1974), 15.

3. Jacques Derrida, *Of Grammatology*, trans. Gayatri Chakravorty Spivak (Baltimore: Johns Hopkins University Press, 1976), 89.
4. Roland Barthes, 'The Death of the Author', in *Image–Music–Text*, trans. Stephen Heath (London: Fontana, 1977), 142–8.
5. Michel Foucault, 'What Is an Author?', in *Aesthetics, Method, and Epistemology: Essential Works of Foucault 1954–1984*, vol. ii, ed. James Faubion, trans. Robert Hurley and others (Harmondsworth: Penguin, 2000), 205–22.
6. Jan Relf, Introduction to John Fowles, *Wormholes: Essays and Occasional Writings*, ed. Jan Relf (London: Vintage, 1999), p. xiii.
7. Raman Selden, Peter Widdowson, and Peter Brooker, *A Reader's Guide to Contemporary Literary Theory*, 4th edn. (London: Prentice-Hall, 1997), 157.
8. Matthew Arnold, *Culture and Anarchy*, ed. J. Dover Wilson (Cambridge: Cambridge University Press, 1960).
9. Linda Hutcheon, *A Poetics of Postmodernism: History, Theory, Fiction* (London: Routledge, 1988), 5.
10. Ibid. 224.
11. Ronald C. Dixon, 'John Fowles', in Larry McCaffery (ed.), *Postmodern Fiction: A Bio-Bibliographical Guide* (New York: Greenwood Press, 1986), 363–6, at 363.
12. Brian McHale, 'Reading Postmodern Artefacts', in Patricia Waugh (ed.), *Postmodernism: A Reader* (London: Edward Arnold, 1992), 211–18, at 211.
13. Hutcheon, *A Poetics of Postmodernism*, 219.
14. Benedict Anderson, *Imagined Communities: Reflections on the Origin and Spread of Nationalism* (London: Verso, 1983), 15; emphasis added.
15. Homi K. Bhabha, 'Signs Taken for Wonders', in Henry Louis Gates Jr. (ed.), *'Race', Writing and Difference* (Chicago: University of Chicago Press, 1986), 163–84, at 172.

CHAPTER 4. LATER PERIOD: 1980–2001

1. Peter Conradi, *John Fowles* (London: Methuen, 1982), 16.
2. Pamela Cooper, *The Fictions of John Fowles: Power, Creativity, Femininity* (Ottawa: University of Ottawa Press, 1991), 193.
3. Bruce Woodcock, *Male Mythologies: John Fowles and Masculinity* (Brighton: Harvester Press, 1984), 24.
4. Judith Butler, *Gender Trouble: Feminism and the Subversion of Identity* (London: Routledge, 1990), 136.
5. Katherine Tarbox, '*The French Lieutenant's Woman* and the Evolution of Narrative', *Twentieth Century Literature*, 42/1 (Spring 1996), 88–102, at 96.

6. Michel Foucault, *The History of Sexuality*, i. *An Introduction*, trans. Robert Hurley (Harmondsworth: Penguin, 1990), 57.
7. Michel Foucault, *The History of Sexuality*, ii: *The Use of Pleasure*, trans. Robert Hurley (Harmondsworth: Penguin, 1992), 3–4.
8. Georg Lukács, *The Historical Novel*, trans. Hannah and Stanley Mitchell (London: Merlin, 1989), 19.
9. Linda Hutcheon, *A Poetics of Postmodernism: History, Theory, Fiction* (London: Routledge, 1988), 57–73.
10. Lukács, *The Historical Novel*, 31.
11. Mikhail Bakhtin, *The Dialogic Imagination*, trans. Caryl Emerson and Michael Holquist (Austin, Tex.: University of Texas Press, 1981), 262.
12. Katherine Tarbox, *The Art of John Fowles* (Athens, Ga.: University of Georgia Press, 1989), 152.
13. William Patrick Day, *In the Circles of Fear and Desire: A Study of Gothic Fantasy* (Chicago: University of Chicago Press, 1985), 44.
14. Daniel Defoe, *Moll Flanders and History of the Devil* (London: Henry G. Bohn, 1854), 458.
15. Daniel Defoe, *Moll Flanders*, ed. David Blewett (Harmondsworth: Penguin, 1989), 364.

Select Bibliography

WORKS BY JOHN FOWLES

Fiction and Poetry

The Collector (London: Jonathan Cape, 1963; London: Vintage, 1998).

The Magus (London: Jonathan Cape, 1966). First published in the USA (Boston: Little, Brown, 1965).

The French Lieutenant's Woman (London: Jonathan Cape, 1969; London: Vintage, 1996).

Poems (New York: Ecco Press, 1973).

The Ebony Tower (London: Jonathan Cape, 1974; London, Vintage, 1997).

The Magus: A Revised Version (London: Jonathan Cape, 1977; London, Vintage, 1997).

Daniel Martin (London: Jonathan Cape, 1977; London: Picador, 1989).

Mantissa (London: Jonathan Cape, 1982).

A Maggot (London: Jonathan Cape, 1985; London, Vintage, 1996).

Non-Fiction and Translations

'Disjoints' (diaries), see unpublished manuscripts entry below.

The Aristos: A Self-Portrait in Ideas (London: Jonathan Cape, 1964). Not to be read before Fowles's fiction, as its style may be offputting, but essential as a handbook of Fowles's early (basically existentialist) philosophy. Published in revised editions with new prefaces as *The Aristos* (London: Jonathan Cape 1968, 1980; London: Triad Grafton, 1981).

Shipwreck, with photographs by the Gibsons of Scilly (London: Jonathan Cape, 1974). Anthologized in *Wormholes*, without the photographs.

Charles Perrault, *Cinderella*, translated by Fowles, illustrated by Sheilah Beckett (London: Jonathan Cape, 1974).

Islands, with photographs by Fay Godwin (London: Jonathan Cape, 1978). A seminal essay about the creative process, which Fowles explores through images of the labyrinth and the voyage. Included in shortened form, without photographs, in *Wormholes*.

Steep Holm – A Case History in the Study of Evolution, co-author Rodney Legg (Sherborne: Kenneth Allsop Memorial Trust, 1978). A tribute to Kenneth Allsop, which adds to Fowles's writings on nature.

The Tree, with preface and photographs by Frank Horvat (London: Aurum Press, 1979). An invaluable account of Fowles's relationship with nature, as well as a meditation on creativity. As important to his middle and later periods as *The Aristos* to his earlier phase. Reissued in paperback without the photographs (London: Vintage, 2000).

The Enigma of Stonehenge, co-author Barry Brukoff (London: Jonathan Cape, 1980). An account of the history of this Ancient British monument, particularly useful to students of *A Maggot*.

A Brief History of Lyme (Lyme Regis: Friends of the Museum, 1981). A short factual account of the town's history.

Land, with photographs by Fay Godwin (London: Heinemann, 1985). Essay on landscape, anthologized in *Wormholes*, without the photographs.

'A Conversation with John Fowles', interviewer Robert Foulke, *Salmagundi* (1985–6), 367–84. Not included in *Conversations with John Fowles*. Develops Fowles's views of the relationship between fiction and history.

'Past and Present Comment: An Afterword', in *Locating the Shakers*, ed. Mick Gidley and Kate Bowles (Exeter: Exeter University Press, 1990), 146–50. Omitted from *Wormholes*, this short but useful essay gives insight into Fowles's construction of the role of the historical novelist.

Claire de Duras, *Ourika, An English Translation*, trans. and foreword by Fowles (New York: Modern Language Association, 1994). *Ourika* and its foreword are important sources for students of *The French Lieutenant's Woman*.

Wormholes: Essays and Occasional Writings, ed. Jan Relf (London: Jonathan Cape, 1998; London: Vintage, 1999). All of Fowles's most important essays – except *The Tree* – under one cover, with a useful summative introduction. Divided into sections on Autobiography, Culture, Literature, and Nature; organized chronologically within sections.

Conversations with John Fowles, ed. Dianne L. Vipond (Jackson: University Press of Mississippi, 1999). Selected interviews from 1963 to 1999, organized chronologically. Not all interviews are as important as others, but this remains an essential document of Fowles's opinions.

Unpublished manuscripts, Harry Ransom Humanities Research Center, The University of Texas at Austin, PO Box 7219, Austin TX 78713-7219, USA. Manuscripts for most of Fowles's published work including *The Magus* and *A Maggot* are held here, plus diaries (called 'Disjoints' by Fowles), letters, and papers from 1944 to 1991, arranged chronologically (mostly in manuscript up to about 1960, mostly in typescript thereafter). Facsimiles of 'Disjoints', the letters, and papers are held at The University of Exeter Library, Stocker Road, Exeter, Devon EX4 4PT, UK.

Film adaptations

The Collector (Columbia Pictures, 1965). Starring Samantha Eggar as Miranda, Terence Stamp as Clegg. Screenplay by Stanley Mann and John Kohn. Directed by William Wyler.

The Magus (20th Century Fox, 1968). Starring Michael Caine as Nicholas Urfe, Anthony Quinn as Conchis, Candice Bergen as Lily. Screenplay by John Fowles. Directed by Guy Green.

The French Lieutenant's Woman (United Artists, 1981). Starring Meryl Streep as Sarah Woodruff, Jeremy Irons as Charles Smithson. Screenplay by Harold Pinter, published as *The Screenplay of 'The French Lieutenant's Woman'* (London: Jonathan Cape, 1981). Directed by Karel Reisz.

The Ebony Tower (Granada Television, 1984). Starring Laurence Olivier as Breasley, Roger Rees as David Williams, Gretta Scacchi as Diana. Screenplay by John Mortimer. Directed by Robert Knights.

BIOGRAPHICAL AND CRITICAL STUDIES

Acheson, James, *John Fowles* (London: Macmillan, 1998). Focuses on Fowles's move away from existentialism. Omits *Mantissa* altogether, but is otherwise extremely useful as a guide to all his main fictions.

Aubrey, James R., *John Fowles: A Reference Companion* (London: Greenwood Press, 1991). An informative short biography plus critical summaries of Fowles's work, a brief account of critical approaches, and a census of Fowles's fictional characters. Explains some unfamiliar terms in the fiction.

—— (ed.), *John Fowles and Nature: Fourteen Perspectives on Landscape* (Madison: Fairleigh Dickinson University Press; London: Associated University Presses, 1999). Essays on landscape, the pastoral, islands, geology, and related matters by leading Fowlesian scholars.

Barnum, Carol M., *The Fiction of John Fowles: A Myth for our Time* (Greenwood, Fla.: Penkevill Publishing Co., 1988). Reads the fictions as contemporary quest myths, using Jungian archetypes. The archetypal scheme connects the texts well; useful for Fowlesians interested in myth and psychology.

Booker, M. Keith, 'What we have instead of God: Sexuality, Textuality and Infinity in *The French Lieutenant's Woman*', *Novel*, 23–4 (Winter 1991), 178–97. Useful on Fowles's parody of Victorian convention and the balance between realism and play in the novel.

Bradbury, Malcolm, 'The Novelist as Impresario: The Fiction of John Fowles', *No, Not Bloomsbury* (London: André Deutsch, 1987), 279–93. Account of Fowles's strengths and weaknesses by another significant novelist.

Butler, Lance St John, 'John Fowles and the Fiction of Freedom', in James Acheson (ed.), *The British and Irish Novel since 1960* (London: Macmillan, 1991), 62–77. Explains Fowles's enigmatic complexity in terms of his relationship to the idea of freedom, in the existentialist and poststructuralist senses.

Conradi, Peter, *John Fowles* (London: Methuen, 1982). A very well-written study of Fowles's early and middle periods.

Cooper, Pamela, *The Fictions of John Fowles: Power, Creativity, Femininity* (Ottawa: University of Ottawa Press, 1991). Feminist reading of Fowles's contradictory treatment of women. Brief on the last three novels but good on Fowles's investigations of creativity and power.

Fawkner, H. W., *The Timescapes of John Fowles* (London: Associated University Presses, 1984). Useful foreword by Fowles. Concentrates narrowly on temporality in Fowles's fiction; a provocative, interdisciplinary study, liked by Fowles.

Harding, Brian, 'Comparative Metafictions of History: E. L. Doctorow and John Fowles', in Ann Massa and Alistair Stead (eds.), *Forked Tongues? Comparing Twentieth-Century British and American Literature* (London: Longman, 1994), 253–72. Helpfully contrasts Fowles's and Doctorow's approaches to history, though not always convincing in its analysis of *A Maggot*.

Huffaker, Robert, *John Fowles* (Boston: Twayne, 1980). Reads Fowles as a naturalist, also examining autobiographical elements in the fiction. First chapter contains a helpful short biography.

Hutcheon, Linda, *A Poetics of Postmodernism: History, Theory, Fiction* (London: Routledge 1988). Places Fowles as a postmodernist, focusing particularly on the meta-fictional qualities of *The French Lieutenant's Woman*.

Journal of Modern Literature, 8/2 (1980–1). Fowles special number. Contains articles on all the novels up to *Daniel Martin*; topics include Fowles's revisions of *The Magus*, the manuscripts of *The French Lieutenant's Woman*, Fowles's philosophy, and theory of play, plus an interview with Raman K. Singh (reproduced in *Conversations with John Fowles*).

Landrum, David W., 'Sarah and Sappho: Lesbian Reference in *The French Lieutenant's Woman*', *Mosaic* 33/1 (Mar. 2000), 59–76. Argues for Sarah's lesbianism – useful for queer perspectives on Fowles.

Loveday, Simon, *The Romances of John Fowles* (Basingstoke: Macmillan, 1985). Argues for Fowles's fictions as incarnations of medieval romance. Appeared too early for *A Maggot* but is particularly clear on *The Magus*.

Modern Fiction Studies, 31/1 (Spring 1985). Fowles special issue. Contains articles on *The Magus, The French Lieutenant's Woman, The Ebony Tower, Daniel Martin*, and *The Tree*, plus Fowles and medieval romance. Also includes a selected checklist of criticism of Fowles, plus an interview with Carol M. Barnum (reproduced in *Conversations with John Fowles*).

Olshen, Barry N., *John Fowles* (New York: Frederick Ungar, 1978). Useful account of Fowles's achievements up to *Daniel Martin*.

Olshen, Barry N., and Olshen, Toni A., *John Fowles: A Reference Guide* (Boston: G. K. Hall, 1980). Now mostly superseded by Aubrey's *Reference Companion* (see above) but still an important source of information on the early work.

Onega, Susana, *Form and Meaning in the Novels of John Fowles* (Ann Arbor: UMI Research Press, 1989). Describes the tension between experimentalism and realism in Fowles's fiction.

Palmer, William J., *The Fiction of John Fowles: Tradition, Art and the Loneliness of Selfhood* (Columbia: University of Missouri Press, 1974). Addresses Fowles's literary influences, his faith in art, and the existentialist themes of his first three novels.

Pifer, Ellen (ed.), *Critical Essays on John Fowles* (Boston: G. K. Hall, 1986). Includes a wide range of essays on Fowles's self-reflexivity and experiments with form, plus philosophy and more esoteric subjects.

Rankin, Elizabeth, 'Cryptic Coloration in *The French Lieutenant's Woman*', *Journal of Narrative Technique*, 3 (1973), 193–207. Situates Fowles's self-reflexive games with reference to the evolution of the novel form. Insightful and provocative.

Rose, Gilbert J., '*The French Lieutenant's Woman*: The Unconscious Significance of a Novel to its Author', *American Imago*, 29 (Summer 1972), 165–76. Important for researchers interested in psychoanalysis and/or gender issues; Fowles drew from it in 'Hardy and the Hag'.

Salami, Mahmoud, *John Fowles's Fiction and the Poetics of Postmodernism* (London: Associated University Presses, 1992). Has an obvious debt to Linda Hutcheon, but particularly useful for students of Fowles interested in literary theory.

Tarbox, Katherine, *The Art of John Fowles* (Athens, Ga.: University of Georgia Press, 1989). Covers the texts chronologically, looking in depth at 'whole sight' and the texts' relationship with the reader, taking a self-consciously heuristic approach.

Twentieth Century Literature, 42/1 (Spring 1996). Fowles special issue. Contains articles on *The Magus*, *The French Lieutenant's Woman*, 'The Ebony Tower', and *Daniel Martin*; other essays cover Fowles's translations (*Ourika* and *Cinderella*) and the Fowles resources at the Harry Ransom Humanities Research Center (see the unpublished manuscripts entry above). Also contains two poems by Fowles, an interview with Dianne L. Vipond, and an essay ('Behind *The Magus*'). The interview and essay are reproduced in *Wormholes*.

Wolfe, Peter, *John Fowles, Magus and Moralist*, 2nd edn., rev. (London: Associated University Presses, 1979). Assesses Fowles's intellectual and moral purposes in the early and middle-period fiction, as well as looking in detail at his language.

Woodcock, Bruce, *Male Mythologies: John Fowles and Masculinity* (Brighton: Harvester Press, 1984). Critiques Fowles's constructions of masculinity, arguing that Fowles's declared feminism conceals the patriarchal bias of his fictions.

Index